Immortality of the Soul

AND

DESTINY OF THE WICKED.

BY THE

Rev. N. L. RICE, D.D.,

President of Westminster College.

PHILADELPHIA:
PRESBYTERIAN BOARD OF PUBLICATION,
1334 CHESTNUT STREET.

WESTCOTT & THOMSON,
Stereotypers, Philada.

PREFACE.

THE following short treatise was commenced several years ago, at the earnest request of the Board of Publication. After the most of it had been written, the entire failure of the writer's health—compelling him to resign his pastoral charge in New York—made it necessary to lay it aside, and until a very recent period the idea of completing it was abandoned. At the renewed request of the Board it has now been finished, and is given to the public with the hope and prayer that, by the divine blessing, it may be of some use in the defence of the truth.

The discussion of the subjects of the Immortality of the Soul and of the Destiny of the Wicked might embrace a very wide range of argument, including extended philosophical investigation and much learned criticism of the original languages of the Scriptures. But the truth of these, like that of all other fundamental doctrines of Christianity, can be satisfactorily demonstrated by a shorter and simpler process. We have written, not with the hope of silencing quibblers or of convincing the prejudiced, but of satisfying sincere inquirers after truth. We have aimed to make the discussion short, plain and convincing. How far we have succeeded we must leave each reader to determine; but we can say truly that, if the arguments employed are unsound, we are wholly unable to detect their unsoundness. We offer to our readers evidences on which our own Christian hopes rest.

IMMORTALITY OF THE SOUL.

CHAPTER I.

STATEMENT OF THE QUESTION.

TWO great questions have, in all ages, excited the anxious inquiries of thinking minds. The first is the question of the introduction of sin and suffering into our world; the second is the question of the continuance of evil, moral and natural. The number and variety of the theories adopted on these subjects sufficiently indicate the difficulties attending the investigation, and show how little satisfaction human reason alone can afford. It is to the second of these two great questions that we propose now to devote a few pages, relying mainly, in the investigation, on the inspired Word, though not neglecting the aid of reason.

That in this world all do sin and suffer, we know; but we inquire anxiously, What is to be the future of man? Will natural and moral evil always continue, or will both terminate either at death or at some future period? Those who regard man as only a material organism, whose conscious existence is terminated by death, of course have no difficulty respecting his eternal future. That which has no conscious existence can be neither holy nor unholy, neither happy nor unhappy. Amongst professing Christians some have held that at the resurrection, though not before, all will be holy and happy. Such is the creed of Universalists. Others think there will be, at least to many, a period of suffering after death, but that ultimately all will be saved. Such is the belief of Restorationists. But the great body of Christians of all ages have believed that after death the righteous will be for ever holy and happy; the wicked for ever unholy and unhappy.

But we are now plausibly urged to abandon the long-established creed of the Church of Christ, and to embrace new doctrines respecting the nature of man and his future. It is contended that evil, natural and moral, must come to an end; that in the government of the infinitely perfect Jehovah, it cannot be eternal. It is further contended that it will terminate, not, as Restorationists and Universalists suppose, by all becoming holy and happy, but by *the annihilation of the wicked.* Those of the human race who die in unbelief, it is affirmed, will, as the just penalty of their sin, return to their original elements, and cease for ever to have a conscious existence. This doctrine has practical bearings far more important than the mere question of the final doom of the wicked, for—

1. It involves the doctrine that the human soul is mortal. One of the most plausible advocates of the annihilation of the wicked

says: "If it were true that immortality is an essential attribute of man, then indeed it must be admitted and maintained that *a* doctrine of endless life in ceaseless woe is a doctrine of the inspired Book." Other advocates of this doctrine contend earnestly that the human soul is not immortal.

2. It involves the doctrine that the human soul is *material*, and, consequently, that man is nothing more than a *material organism*. We propose, in the progress of this discussion, to prove that Annihilationists do teach this doctrine. They cannot escape from it; for if the soul is pure spirit, it is not subject to decay or decomposition.

3. Logically it involves the denial of the doctrine of man's free and accountable agency, and, consequently, the denial of the possibility of sin and holiness in man. For matter, being governed by fixed laws, is incapable of voluntary action, and, of course, incapable of moral action. This is not an inference of ours. The two doctrines—materialism and

human accountability—have never, so far as we know, been associated for any length of time.

The history of the sensational philosophy, which gained a wonderful popularity in France just before the Revolution, warns us of the inevitable tendencies of the doctrine of the materiality of the soul. The leading philosophers of that period regarded man as a mere material organism, but for a time they shrank from carrying out the doctrine to its logical results. Men, however, are far more likely to carry out false principles, even to the most revolting results, than to abandon them and return to the truth. The time soon came when the philosophers of France, having asserted the materiality of the soul, denied its free agency, and made virtue and vice synonymous with pleasure and pain. 'The crowning piece,' says the learned Morell, 'in which the ultimate results of the whole system are concentrated, was presented to the world by the Baron d'Holbach in his "Système de la Nature," a work in which materialism, fatalism and avowed atheism all combine to form a view of human nature which even Voltaire pronounced to be illogical in its deductions, absurd in its physics and abominable in its morality.' "—*Hist. of Mod. Philos.*, v. i., p. 161.

4. Logically it also involves the rejection of a vicarious atonement. The doctrine, inconsistent with itself, is, that man is mortal by nature; that he would, therefore, die by the course of nature, and death would be the endurance of the entire penalty of his sin, if we suppose him capable of sinning. If, after this, God were pleased to raise him from his dust to a new life, only the exertion of infinite power would be necessary; and there appears to be no reason why the incarnation and death of Christ should be necessary in order to the putting forth of such power. We are not surprised, therefore, to find one of the most plausible advocates of annihilationism rejecting and contending against the

doctrine. He says: "In two different ways is the actual pardon of sin denied—1st. Where sin is said to be punished in the person of the transgressor. 2d. Where it is said to be punished in the person of the Redeemer." Again: "We remark, then, that it [the doctrine that sin was punished in the Redeemer] seems to be implied and properly to inhere in several of the theodicies of eternal suffering." And again: "That theory of the atonement which makes the sufferings of Christ a satisfaction to the divine justice is commonly found in closest connection with the notion of sin as infinite guilt." * We quote this language, not now for the purpose of refuting it, but simply to show that according to this writer the two doctrines—the eternal punishment of the wicked and the vicarious atonement of Christ—stand or fall together.

5. If the preceding positions are true, it requires no long argument to prove that the prevalence of the doctrines of annihila-

* "Debt and Grace," pp. 392–397.

tionists must result in the overthrow of morals. In making man a mere material organism and denying his free agency, they furnish the very best apology for all wickedness; and in making the only penalty of sin the privation of conscious existence, they take away one of the most powerful motives by which it is restrained. It may be said that men shrink from annihilation more than from eternal suffering. But, in the first place, the zeal with which not a few in our day are seeking to prove, scientifically, that man is only a material and perishing organism, disproves the assertion. In the second place, it is an instructive fact that it was when the French infidels of the Revolution succeeded in convincing the masses of the people that death is an eternal sleep, that wickedness in every form abounded, and France became a pandemonium.

If, then, we have not misunderstood the consequences which legitimately flow from the doctrine of annihilationism, it is evidently of sufficient importance to demand careful investigation. Should we embrace this doctrine, we do not merely abandon one of the doctrines of our present creed. We receive a doctrine which will, if we are consistent, compel us to reject other doctrines hitherto regarded as fundamental to the Christian system; nor is it easy to say where we should find a solid resting-place for our faith.

It is, then, apparent that the discussion of the doctrine of the annihilation of the wicked involves the inquiry into the nature as well as the destiny of man. The following questions will cover the entire ground of the discussion, and will conduct us without confusion through the several steps necessary to a safe and satisfactory conclusion:

I. What do the Scriptures teach us respecting the nature of the soul?

II. How far do the known properties of the soul confirm the obvious meaning of the Scriptures respecting its nature?

III. What do the Scriptures teach us respecting the state of the soul between death and the resurrection?

IV. What do the Scriptures teach respecting the eternal state of the wicked?

CHAPTER II.

PRELIMINARY CONSIDERATIONS.

BEFORE entering upon the discussion of these questions, there are some preliminary considerations which claim attention, either as affording strong presumptive evidence against the annihilationist creed, or as removing difficulties and preparing the way for a satisfactory discussion of the whole subject.

1. It is important to explain the sense in which the word *immortality* is employed in relation to the soul. In the New Testament there are two words translated *immortality*—*aphtharsia* and *athanasia*. In the highest sense these words are applied to God. In 1 Tim. i. 7 we read: "Now unto the King eternal, immortal (*aphtharto*), invisible, the

only wise God, be honor and glory for ever." In 1 Tim. vi. 16 we read: "Who only hath immortality (*athanasian*), dwelling in light which no man can approach unto." Now, it is manifest that immortality cannot belong to any finite being in the sense in which it belongs to God. Of him only can it be said that he "hath life in himself." The immortality of a creature must of necessity be derived and dependent.

These words are used with reference to the bodies of the saints as they will be raised from the dead. In 1 Cor. xv. 53 it is written: "For this corruptible must put on incorruption (*aphtharsian*), and this mortal must put on immortality (*athanasian*)." Their bodies will be so changed and refined as to be no more subject to decay and death. The word *aphtharsia* is also employed to express the happy immortality of the righteous. Rom. ii. 7. The English word *immortality* is constantly used to signify the incorruptibility of the soul, in consequence of which it does not die with the body, but will live for ever. Webster defines it to be "the quality of being immortal; exemption from death and annihilation; life destined to endure without end." In this sense we use the word when we affirm that the soul is immortal. We do not mean that it possesses an immortality independent of its Creator, or that he could not, if he chose, annihilate it, but that, as he designed it to live for ever, he imparted to it a nature suited to its destiny. Whether the word *immortality* is applied to the soul in this sense in the Scriptures or not, the doctrine which it expresses we hope to prove is abundantly taught there.

2. That the Scriptures do teach this doctrine is made extremely probable—to use no stronger language—by the fact that the church of Christ in all ages and countries has so understood them. Hudson, one of the most plausible advocates of the soul's mortality, asserts that the early history of the opposite doctrine "is evidently Platonic," and he adds:

"This view was first tolerated in the Christian church in the person of a remarkable man in the fifth century, Synesius." But, in the first place, the doctrine of Plato, as stated by this author himself, is essentially different from that which we advocate. He says: "Plato himself regarded the soul as not only immortal, but a divine essence, and, because divine, it was pre-existent and eternal." But we who contend for the doctrine of the soul's immortality do not regard it as a divine essence, or as pre-existent, but as simply created by God with a nature not subject to decay and death. Our doctrine, therefore, is not of Platonic origin. Besides, this same author informs us that Justin Martyr, in his "Exhortation to the Greeks," mentions the doctrine "of the soul's immortality" among the truths "held in common by the philosophers and the Christians." * Now, Justin Martyr lived in the *second century* of the Christian era, and no man had better opportunities of

* "Debt and Grace," p. 313.

knowing the faith of Christians at that period. It cannot be true, then, that the doctrine of the soul's immortality was first tolerated in the Christian church in the *fifth* century. The truth is, that the doctrines of the soul's mortality and of the annihilation of the wicked never gained a footing in the primitive church.

We have a very important testimony respecting the belief of the church in all its branches, for several centuries past, which relieves us from the necessity of adducing other proofs. One of the ablest annihilationists says: "From the various schools of ecclesiastical tuition a reply [*i. e.*, to the question, *What is man?*] has come forth, the substance of which may be thus condensed: 'Man is an immortal being'—mortal as to his body, but immortal in his soul." And after stating the doctrine of the future destiny of the wicked, he says: "From the press and from the pulpit the reply has for centuries gone forth. In every country in Christendom, and in every city and hamlet, this teaching is heard." * We are far from claiming infallibility for the church in her interpretations of the Scriptures, but we are as far from regarding it as even remotely probable that on a subject of so great importance—a subject of which, confessedly, the Scriptures treat abundantly and plainly—the whole church has been given up for centuries to believe a lie. We are constrained to ask, What strange and all-pervading delusion has come over the minds of all the students of God's word—embracing great multitudes of the eminently wise and good—that for centuries past they should have so grossly misinterpreted its plain language, all, too, understanding it in the same way? Within these centuries the Scriptures have been in the hands of the people, and have been studied as never before by learned laymen—independent thinkers—as well as by learned ministers, and during no preceding period have

* "Question of Ages," p. 381.

the minds of good men been so free from the perverting influence of false philosophy. The Reformation expelled Plato and Aristotle from the church, but the doctrine of the soul's immortality remained. The Baconian philosophy gave a new direction to philosophical inquiry, but still this doctrine has held its place in the creed of almost the whole of Christendom. How shall we account for this if the doctrine is false and injurious? Is it more probable that the whole church should have so long and so strangely erred, or that the few men who now assail the long-established faith have themselves misinterpreted the inspired record? We leave the candid reader to answer. But surely we are justified in demanding of those who make pretensions so extraordinary, arguments the most conclusive, before we change our faith.

3. On close inspection we discover in the creed we are invited to embrace some inconsistencies which shake our confidence in it. The truth is always consistent with itself, and

the human understanding refuses to receive contradictions as inspired truths.

1st. The annihilationist creed ascribes the same qualities to two substances essentially different in their nature. Annihilationists hold that the soul is a material substance, and that God is a spirit, and so are angels; and yet they ascribe the same qualities or properties to these two essentially different substances. We may be charged with misrepresentation when we charge them with holding that the soul is matter. Let us, therefore, adduce the evidence upon which the statement is founded. Hudson, shrinking from the avowal of gross materialism, yet admits "the prevalence of a materialist philosophy which has frequently attended the doctrine we (annihilationists) maintain;" and he insists, in the behalf of pious materialists, "that speculative materialism is not to be for itself condemned." * Now, between the doctrine that the soul is spirit, and the doctrine

* "Debt and Grace," pp. 243, 246.

that the soul is matter, there is fundamental difference. The one view or the other is a very grave error. Why, then, we may reasonably inquire, has a materialist philosophy so frequently attended the doctrine of annihilationism, unless there is some decided affinity between the two? Evidently the advocates of this doctrine have felt that the spiritual nature of the soul could never be made to harmonize with it. And why, we may further ask, is not speculative materialism to be for itself condemned if it be an error? Is not all error, especially on a subject so vital, injurious? But our author himself, whilst apparently contending that the soul is "a spiritual substance," adopts a theory which is substantially and really materialistic. His theory is that "which regards the soul as an entity, not destroyed by the death of the body, however dependent it may be on an embodiment for the purposes of active existence." * No materialist imagines that death destroys

* "Debt and Grace," p. 250.

either body or soul, *as an entity*. If conscious existence is destroyed, it avails nothing to say that as an entity the soul still exists. If it does not exist as an intelligent, active being, it is virtually destroyed. To speak of its condition as "a repose"—"not a state of thinking, perhaps, on the other hand, not of unconsciousness, but of momentary all-consciousness" *—is to use words without meaning. It is the attempt to imagine a state unknown alike to philosophy and to the Scriptures.

Another writer of the same school, shrinking from the avowal of materialism, admits that the soul is a *substance*, yet denies that it is either matter or spirit. In one place he speaks of "the vital, vigorous substance, the *immaterial* soul of man," as created by God. In another place, replying to the argument that the soul is immaterial, and therefore immortal, he says: "The argument is invalid and unreasonable, and its only supposable

* "Debt and Grace," p. 261.

force arises from a silent assumption that because the soul of man *is not matter*, therefore *it is spirit*. But this assumption is not warranted." * Now, since the soul is confessedly a substance, it must be either matter or spirit, unless there is a third substance different in nature from both of these. There is no third substance known to us, and, therefore, if the soul is not spirit, we must regard it as matter. And notwithstanding the occasional use of language which might have another meaning, this is evidently the view of our author, for he contends that man is wholly of earthly origin. The sentence pronounced upon Adam he expounds thus: "In the sweat of thy face shalt THOU eat bread, till THOU return into the earth; for out of it (MIMENHA—out of that sort of origin) wast THOU taken: for dust (GAH-PHAR, elemental atoms) THOU art, and unto dust (elemental atoms) shalt THOU return." He adds by way of comment: "In this sentence pronounced on the man, the *fact* of

* "Quest. of Ages," pp. 5, 27.

his personal origin out of the earth is embodied." * Now, dust is matter; and he who contends that man, as a person, is formed of dust, and at death returns to dust, is a materialist.

Another writer of the same creed reasons about the immateriality of the soul thus: "Where is the proof that the soul is immaterial? It certainly is not drawn from nature, for all nature is material; it is not drawn from reason, for reason cannot comprehend the existence of immateriality; it cannot be drawn from revelation, for that expressly declares that *man is dust* and the mind carnal." † Can there be grosser materialism or more absurd reasoning than this? Yet the writer, as if, under the silent protest of his own soul, shrinking from his own doctrine, says: "We do not mean to be understood that the mind is material, but we do claim that all vital and mental phenomena result from material causes." Then take

* "Quest. of Ages," p. 34.

† "Mortal or Immortal," p. 25.

away the material causes, and all vital and mental phenomena must cease. Where, then, is the soul, and what is it? He has explained his meaning in replying to the argument for the immateriality of the soul founded in Eccles. xii. 7. The word translated *spirit*, he contends, means *breath*, and he reasons thus: "Is, then, this breath of life the spirit which God has given to man? We have no record of any other. But this breath of life, as we have seen, is common to all living things," * etc. The soul of man, then, is only his breath, and just such souls have all living things! There can be no grosser materialism than this.

Now, according to the creed of these writers, God is a *spirit*, and the soul of man is *matter*. What are the properties of spirit as they appear in the divine nature? They are intelligence, voluntary agency and moral character. God is an infinitely intelligent Being, he is infinitely free in his choices

* "Mortal or Immortal," p. 40.

and acts, and he is infinitely holy. These are the distinguishing properties of spirit. But the soul of man, though finite, is an intelligent being, free in its choices and acts, and possesses moral character. Possessing, therefore, the distinguishing properties of spirit, it is spirit. There is no greater absurdity than to ascribe the same properties to two substances essentially different in nature. This absurdity is chargeable upon the doctrine we are controverting. The ancient Sadducees, who denied the immortality of the soul, were consistent enough to deny the existence of spirits. "For the Sadducees say that there is no resurrection, neither angel nor spirit." * But the annihilationists are inconsistent enough to maintain the materiality and mortality of the soul, and yet to admit the existence of spirits.

2d. The creed of the annihilationists is absurd and contradictory, because, according to it, the righteous, though they are justified,

* Acts xxiii. 8.

suffer the full penalty of sin *once*, the wicked, *twice*. They insist with great earnestness that "the revealed penalty of human sin, and, in this, the revealed destiny of man, as a sinner, is found in the sentence pronounced upon Adam," which, as interpreted by one of them, means that man was formed of *the dust*—elemental atoms—and is to return to dust or elemental atoms. "The first man," says he, "is out of the earth, and the final destiny of man, as man and a sinner, is to return unto the earth, and to become as though he had not been. The destiny of man, as denounced of God in the garden of Eden, is continuously shown in the concurrent teaching of the inspired Book."* Now, if it be true that the soul is material and dies with the body, every human being does suffer this entire penalty at death, for then the entire person returns to dust or elemental atoms. It is true that the writer just quoted attempts to escape the difficulty by saying that,

* "Quest. of Ages," pp. 34, 135.

since Jesus died and rose again, "the saints do not in reality die, but, before that, the saints died and were held captive by death."* But this assertion, if it were true, does not remove the difficulty; for it would still be true that the saints who died before the death and resurrection of Christ did suffer the full penalty of sin; for their souls, as we are told, were "held by the chords of death insensible and inert." But other annihilationists do not accept this theory, that since the resurrection of Christ the saints do not die. One of them states his belief thus: "That man has no inherent immortal principle in his nature. That consequently no part of him remains in a separate conscious state in death, but that the whole man lies in unconsciousness till called to new life by the resurrection." † Accordingly, he labors to prove that all those passages which seem to teach that the saints, between the time of

* Quest. of Ages," p. 107.

† Preface to "Mortal or Immortal."

their death and that of the resurrection, enjoy a happy existence, mean something else. Hudson reasons in the same way.

The penalty of sin, then, according to annihilationists, is death—that is, the return of man, soul and body, to the earth from which he was taken. If this is the penalty, every one who dies suffers it. But the saints die and return to dust. Therefore the saints endure the full penalty of sin. This conclusion is not affected by the fact, if it were true, that new beings will, at some distant period, be created out of the same "elemental atoms," for in no possible sense could they be the same persons who died. And if this were possible, still it would be true that they did suffer the whole penalty when they returned to dust. Hudson sees and vainly attempts to escape the difficulty respecting *identity*. He says: "This view [*i. e.*, that the soul dies with the body] makes the identity of man's present and future being inexplicable, if not impossible." He would meet the difficulty by the theory, already noticed, that the soul continues as "an entity," though without active existence. His view of the penalty, consequently, is stated thus: "In the doctrine of death which we maintain, this view of man's nature would lead us to say that the first and second death are the first and second installments of the debt incurred by sin, the execution of the sentence being divided in such sort that those who escape the second death are in the New Testament spoken of not as properly dead, but as fallen asleep."* But, in the first place, this view is absurd. The soul is either matter or spirit. If it is matter, death destroys it as completely as it destroys the body. If it is spirit, death simply dissolves the tie that binds soul and body together, and it passes into another state of conscious existence. A spirit must possess the properties of spirit, and therefore must be active, thinking, feeling, acting. To talk of the disembodied soul as "lost in

* "Debt and Grace," pp. 247, 250.

an intuition of its past history, with no process of thinking and with no note of time," is to talk nonsense.* Neither philosophy nor revelation knows anything of such a state.

Secondly, If we were to admit the truth of these wild conjectures, and that the penalty of sin is divided into "two installments," still, the righteous, as well as the wicked, would pay the first installment. Now, the Scriptures teach us that believers in Christ are fully justified, and that to them "there is no condemnation." † They suffer no part of the penalty of sin. They are, indeed, subject to natural death, but in the case of believers the plan of redemption has converted death into a rich blessing, since it introduces them into the blissful presence of God. Paul, therefore, in enumerating the believer's blessings, includes death among them. ‡ But according to the doctrine of annihilationists, death deprives the righteous,

* "Debt and Grace," p. 261. † Rom. viii. 1.
‡ 1 Cor. iii. 22.

as well as the wicked, of conscious existence; it converts them into "elemental atoms," or dust. They, therefore, suffer just what was denounced against Adam as the penalty of sin. So that we have, in the case of the righteous, the same persons fully justified, yet enduring the penalty of sin. This is contradiction.

But as for the wicked, they endure the penalty *twice*, which is absurd, and would be unjust. For the advocates of annihilation tell us that after having died once—having returned to dust—they are to be raised from the dead that they may again be annihilated, or die a second time! Hudson saw the difficulty, and it had its influence in inducing him to adopt the absurd theory of the soul's continued existence as "an entity." Says he, "If the human soul or spirit is not an immaterial substance, but perishes with the body, then the wicked will wholly die twice, and the penalty of the law will appear to be executed a second time. This difficulty, with another to be named hereafter, has led many to deny that the 'resurrection of the unjust' signifies their being made alive." To such absurdities are men driven who abandon the obvious teachings of God's word.*

Another advocate of annihilation seeks to remove this difficulty. "Adam," he says, "has suffered the penalty of his first transgression, death. Death temporal—or rather, we should say, death temporary—is entailed in consequence upon all our race. And had not the plan of salvation immediately supervened upon the fall, this would have been the end of Adam and his posterity, for we have already seen that death is a state of non-existence, and the only avenue there is from that land of dark unconsciousness back to life is through the resurrection, which is effected by Christ." But we are to answer, he tells us, "for our personal acts and transgressions." For this purpose we are all to

* "Debt and Grace," p. 247.

have a future life. And if, then, there are found remaining against us sins unrepented of and unforgiven, what will be our sentence? Answer: The same fearful sentence which has everywhere, from first to last, been pronounced against sin, "The soul that sinneth it shall *die*."* But how is this? These writers do most earnestly insist that the penalty of sin is death—that is, the return of man, body and soul, to dust. If this is the penalty of sin, then, when a man dies he fully endures the penalty due to all his sin. How is it, then, that he is to be created over again, that he may again endure the same sentence? It is useless to tell us that the first death is *entailed*, since we are assured that it is the precise penalty of sin. There is no escape from the conclusion that, according to the annihilationist creed, the wicked are to suffer the penalty of the law *twice*. We need no stronger evidence that it is untrue.

* "Mortal or Immortal," pp. 104, 105.

But let us look at this point again. As already shown, these writers tell us that the penalty of sin is death; and yet some of them seem to teach that death or annihilation is a merciful arrangement, not an infliction of the penalty. One of them, giving his creed, states the matter thus: "That the wicked will be punished in a future state, that they will be rewarded every man according to his deeds, but that they will receive this punishment at the hands of a God whose *mercy* is co-equal with his *justice*, and who will suffer them to go back to their original elements and cease from existence, as entitled to no name nor place in all the universe of God." * Now, according to the view here given, the penalty of sin is to be endured in the future state, and after the wicked shall have fully endured that penalty, God, who is as merciful as he is just, will *permit* them to become extinct. Annihilation, therefore, is the merciful termination of their sufferings, not the

* Pref. to "Mortal or Immortal."

punishment of their sins. Now, both of these views cannot be true. If the annihilation of the wicked is "the fearful sentence which has everywhere, from first to last, been pronounced against sin," it cannot be a merciful permission to the wicked to return to the original elements out of which they were formed.

But, after all, can it be true that death or annihilation is, in any sense, the penalty of sin? Let us examine. In the first place, we are assured that man was created mortal, but had the offer of immortality on certain conditions. "Though not immortal, he was capable of living to perpetuity, and this constitutional life, possessed as the gift of his Creator, he held unsubject to death on the sole condition of non-disobedience to the prohibitory command which his Creator had imposed." * Man, then, was mortal, but on certain conditions he might have lived for ever. He chose not to comply with those conditions, and consequently, being mortal, he

* "Quest. of Ages," p. 32.

must perish, in the natural course of things. The gospel makes to him another offer of immortality on other conditions. If he declines the offer, being mortal, he dies. "The gospel offers him everything, and invites—with all the earnestness of divine love it urges—his acceptance. But it obtrudes upon him nothing." * Now, according to this view, death is not a penalty at all. Man was mortal. He had the offer of immortality, but did not accept. He therefore continued to be mortal, and must die without the necessity of any divine infliction. The gospel, again, offers immortality. Some accept and will live for ever. Others either never hear the offer or decline it, and therefore, being mortal, they die, in the course of nature. If they should be newly created or raised from the dead, they must be raised mortal or immortal. If they are raised mortal, they will again die, in course of nature. If immortal, they will not be annihilated. Anni-

* "Debt and Grace," p. 7.

hilation, therefore, instead of being the infliction of a "fearful sentence," must be a mere natural result. True, death might be hastened by divine judgments, but in this world the wicked often live as long as or longer than the righteous. The truth is, this creed is a bundle of contradictions and absurdities. The different parts of it cannot be reconciled with each other. It rests on neither a philosophical nor a scriptural foundation. It cannot be true.

4. The modes of defending their creed adopted by annihilationists can lead only to error. They are modes by which any doctrine of the Scriptures might be successfully assailed, or any error successfully defended. We now call attention to two of their peculiarities.

1st. They make a great deal out of the fact that certain terms and phrases now employed by believers in the soul's immortality are not found in the Scriptures. One of them states the number of times the words translated *soul* and *spirit* are found in the Bible, and glories in "the stupendous fact" that in no instance is it called an *immortal* or a *deathless* soul.

The whole force of this vaunted argument consists in the fact that the words *immortal* and *deathless* are not found in the Bible connected with the words *soul* and *spirit.* Now, suppose we should urge, as a triumphant refutation of the doctrine of the *mortality* of the soul, another "stupendous fact" which this dashing writer seems to have overlooked, viz.: that in all those hundreds of instances in which the words *soul* and *spirit* occur, the soul is never once denominated *mortal,* nor the spirit called *dying.* If the absence of the words *immortal* and *deathless* proves that the soul is not immortal, does not the absence of the words *mortal* and *dying* prove as clearly that it is not mortal? This mode of arguing would prove that the soul is neither mortal nor immortal. A wise man never uses arguments against the creed of others which are fatal to his own.

But if, as this writer affirms, the silence of the Scriptures is *significant*, may not its meaning be the reverse of what he supposes? It is a fact that, in the days of Christ and his apostles, the doctrine of the immortality of the soul prevailed amongst the Jews, and also amongst the Gentiles. The Sadducees denied it, but the Pharisees, who were much more numerous, held it. If, then, this doctrine is erroneous and injurious, should we not expect to find, in some of the numerous instances in which the words *soul* and *spirit* occur in the New Testament, the soul denominated *mortal* and the spirit *dying?* Would they allow such an error, so prevalent, to go unrebuked? If, then, this silence is significant, it bears hardly on the doctrine of the annihilationists.

But all such reasoning is shallow and deceptive. It confounds two totally different things, viz.: the silence of the Scriptures in relation to *the doctrine* of the soul's immortality, and the absence from the Scriptures of certain *words* and *phrases* now employed to express this doctrine. Why may it not be taught by means of other words and phrases? Suppose the inspired account of the creation of man should prove that his soul is *spirit*, not *matter*. Suppose the Scriptures should teach that at death the soul passes into another state of conscious existence, that the righteous are happy in the presence of God, the wicked unhappy in outer darkness. Suppose we learn from the inspired volume that after the resurrection the wicked will suffer for ever. Would not the doctrine of the immortality of the soul be as clearly taught in these ways as if the words *immortal* and *deathless* were used? Who does not know that in all ages theological writers have adopted words and phrases to express Scripture truths, which words and phrases are not in the Scriptures? The word *trinity*, the phrases *total depravity*, *perseverance of the saints*, and the like, are not found in the Scriptures; but does it follow that the doctrines thus expressed are not there? The annihilationists themselves make free use of terms which are not scriptural. The advocates of truth never find it necessary to resort to this shallow mode of argumentation.

2d. Whilst asserting with great positiveness the meaning of those passages of Scripture which, as they think, favor their views, the annihilationists labor to make the meaning of those passages which teach the opposite doctrines, *perfectly doubtful.* For example, the sentence pronounced on Adam, it is very positively asserted, teaches that the whole man, body and soul, dies. But when Solomon, speaking of death, says, "Then shall the dust return to the earth as it was, and the spirit shall return unto God who gave it," they labor only to render the meaning of his language perfectly doubtful. One of them replies to the argument from this passage thus: "This argument is based on the assumption that the word translated 'spirit' in the above passage is used as a substantive noun, and means the *soul* of man. But this is not self-evident, and may not be the meaning at all. The original word, RUAH, may possibly mean the breath of man, as in Gen. vi. 17 and several other places. We do not say that, in this instance, it means the breath. It may be used to signify the *motion* of the soul in passing away, and passing into the custody of God. . . . The doctrine deducible from the text may be this." * This passage is one of the most important in the Bible, as explaining the sentence pronounced upon man after the fall. This very critical writer is entirely positive in giving to the language of that sentence an interpretation widely different from that of all respectable critics and commentators; but when he comes to an inspired explanation of it, he can only discover that it *may* mean this, or it *may* mean that, and the doctrine it teaches *may* be so and so! What can such criticism do but mislead? The language of Solomon *has* a meaning, and

* "Quest. of Ages," p. 18.

it is the business of those who undertake to expound it, to ascertain what it *does* mean, not what it *may* mean.

Again, when our Lord bade his disciples "fear him which is able to destroy both soul and body in hell," the advocates of annihilation are positive as to his meaning: the word *destroy* of course means *annihilate.* But when he says to the penitent thief, "Verily I say unto thee, To-day shalt thou be with me in Paradise," they tell us his language *may* mean either of several things. One author says: "The meaning may be, I say unto thee, Even this day, when it all seems so unlikely, thou shalt be with me in Paradise, when I enter my kingdom, or the term Paradise may denote the state of the saints in the underworld." * Another writer of the same creed proposes three interpretations of our Lord's language, and gravely says: "There is a degree of plausibility in each. The reader can adopt that which seems to him most satis-

* "Debt and Grace," p. 257.

factory, but if he should have the curiosity to inquire which the writer was inclined to regard as the truthful one, he would be told the first." * In connection with this passage, the writer makes a truly characteristic remark. He says: "We would just as soon suggest several explanations of the same scripture as we would several methods of solving the same problem, provided they all equally get the answer." † Precisely so. A certain "answer" is desired, and the question is, not what the language of particular texts really means, but how they may be interpreted so as to get the desired answer!

Again, in noticing the argument from 2 Cor. v. 8 and Phil. i. 21–23, Hudson says: "The phrase, 'to be absent from the body,' may therefore denote, not the happiness of a disembodied state, but a release from the suffering and dying body, either to 'sleep in Jesus,' or to be present with Christ in the glorified body of the resurrection. . . . When

* "Mortal or Immortal," p. 57. † Ibid., p. 51.

he then adds, 'To live is Christ, and to die is gain,' he may signify either the gain to the cause of Christ by the martyrdom which in his prison he awaited, or his own greater reward, as a martyr, in the resurrection. . . . And as in the other passage, so here, the departure to be with Christ may denote either the repose of the saints in the bosom of Christ, or the full union with him in the resurrection which Paul so earnestly desires." *

These writers seem perfectly satisfied when they have said, respecting any passage of Scripture that stands in their way, that it *may* mean something widely different from the meaning almost universally attributed to it. This is the abuse of criticism. There is no important word that has not several meanings; and therefore there are few texts of Scripture to which several different interpretations may not be plausibly given. It is the business of interpreters, not to try to evade the plain meaning of Scripture language

* "Debt and Grace," p. 256.

by saying, it *may* mean something different, but to ascertain *what it does in fact mean.* Whilst there are passages that are obscure, concerning the meaning of which there may be doubt, those just noticed are not of this class. The language is plain, and interpreters are very generally agreed respecting the true interpretation of them. Let us take not a part, but all that Scriptures say of the soul of man and his destiny, and let it be our aim to ascertain the true meaning of each class of texts, and the doctrine taught by the whole, not to discover what interpretation *may* be forced upon them. Thus, and only thus, can we hope to arrive at the truth.

CHAPTER III.

THE CREATION OF MAN.

WE are now prepared to inquire, *To what conclusion does the inspired account of the creation of man conduct us respecting the nature of the soul?* The account, though very brief, does not leave us in the dark on this point.

In the first place, we notice a very striking difference between the history of the creation of the different orders of animals and that of the creation of man. Concerning certain classes of animals, God said, "Let the waters bring forth abundantly the moving creature that hath life." Concerning other classes, he said, "Let the earth bring forth the living creature after his kind." The language is as if they were exclusively of earthly origin and nature. But when man was to be created, neither the waters nor the earth were commanded to produce him. There was counsel in heaven, and God said, "Let us make man." "And the Lord God formed man of the dust of the ground, and breathed into his nostrils the breath of life, and man became a living soul." Whatever criticisms may be resorted to respecting the phrases, "breath of life," and "living soul," it is certain, from the account of the creation of man, that he is a being of very far nobler nature and higher destiny than the various orders of animals.

But, secondly, it is the glory of man that he was created *in the image of God.* "And God said, Let us make man in our image, after our likeness. So God created man in his own image, in the image of God created he him, male and female created he them." Here arises one of the most important inquiries in the whole discussion, viz.: what is the image and likeness of God in which man was created?

The image was *corporeal,* says one annihilationist writer. It is almost incredible that any man with the Bible in his hand should embrace an error so gross and so impious. But hear his language: "But it is urged that man cannot be in the image of God in respect to bodily form, for God is without form, body or parts. A grand mistake, reader, and one that has not been without its weight in giving rise to the interpretation of Gen. i. 26, already refuted." And after making what he regards as an argument, he concludes thus: "And there is no definition given to the word (image) when applied to a material object like man, which will allow us to refer it to anything else but the outward shape, the physical contour. We hence conclude that Gen. i. 27 simply informs us that in this respect man resembled his Maker."* It cannot be necessary, in this

* "Mortal or Immortal," pp. 10–12.

day, and in this country, to expose an error so exceedingly gross. Paul tells us that when men became fools they "changed the glory of the incorruptible God into an image made like to corruptible man;" and therefore God abandoned them.* We need no better evidence of the truth of the doctrine of the immortality of the soul than the fact, if it be a fact, that the opposite doctrine can be sustained only by degrading the Creator of all.

Another writer of the same class says: "We know that the image of God, in which man was made, was not corporeal, for GOD IS SPIRIT." But he asks, "Why should it be questioned that the image of God, in which man was made, was *governmental*, and only governmental? The delegation of dominion is the predominant thought in the passage," † etc. We answer:

1. To make the image merely governmental is inconsistent with the inspired account. It is certain that "the delegation of do-

* Rom. i. 22, 23. † "Quest. of Ages," p. 14.

minion" over inferior creatures could not take place till after man was created, but it is expressly declared that God *created man in his image.* It was in the act of creation, not in the after act of delegating dominion, that the image of God was imparted. The image, therefore, belongs to the soul, and does not consist in any extraneous thing. The fact that man bore the image of God was the reason why he had authority over the animal creation, but the image is one thing, the authority, another.

In the first Epistle to the Corinthians the apostle speaks of the man, in contrast with the woman, as "the image and glory of God," and this language is understood to refer to delegated authority.* But this is not inconsistent with the common interpretation of the passage under consideration; for it has been well remarked, "When, in Gen. i. 26, 27, it is said, God created man in his own image, the reference is as much to woman as to man,

* 1 Cor. xi. 7.

for it is immediately added, 'Male and female created he them.' "*

2. The Scriptures abundantly confirm the obvious meaning of the inspired account of man's creation, that the image of God belongs to the soul itself, and they leave no room to doubt in what that image consists. One of the annihilationist authors gives us some curious criticisms on the original Hebrew. The word translated *likeness*, he informs us, "is very general in its meaning, implying some kind of equivalence, either in the way of reality or of representation;" and with this statement he dismisses the word, leaving his readers to discover, if they can, what kind of "equivalence" it implies in the passage he is interpreting. The word translated *image*, he says, "signifies an image or representation that may be compared, but *must* also be contrasted, with the object which it is designed to represent." He refers us to Ezek. xvi. 17 and Ps. xxxix. 6, and suc-

* Dr. Hodge, in Loco.

ceeds in reaching the conclusion that *image* means a *shadow*—that "man at first was only the image or shadow of God"—"the *life* of man was but the *shadow* of the *immortality* of God." *

There can be no greater abuse of the principles of language than such criticism as this. The words translated "likeness" and "image," like all other important words, have very different meanings when applied to different things. The question before us is this: What do these words mean when used to express the likeness of one intelligent being to another? And the only way to obtain a satisfactory answer to this question is to examine other passages in which these words are used to express *such* likeness. Now, in neither of the passages referred to by this writer is the word translated *image* used for such purpose. The subjects to which it relates are wholly different; and it would be as wise to quote a passage that speaks of the

* "Quest. of Ages," pp. 13, 14.

head of a *nail*, in order to ascertain the meaning of the word *head* as applied to a man, as to refer to those passages to determine what is the image of God in which man was created.

Both the words in question are found in Gen. v. 3, where it is said, Adam "begat a son in his own likeness, after his image." Is the word *likeness* here "very general in its meaning, implying some kind of equivalence"? Does the word *image* here signify "a representation that may be compared, but *must* also be contrasted, with the object it is designed to represent"? Was Seth merely the *shadow* of his father? The unlearned reader is at no loss to understand the meaning of these words as here used; and the obvious meaning here will help us to explain their meaning in the passage we are examining.

In the Septuagint the Hebrew word for *image* is translated by the Greek word *eikon*, and this last word is repeatedly used in the New Testament to express the image of God.

In Col. i. 15, Jesus Christ is said to be "the image of the invisible God." It will scarcely be pretended that here the word *image* means *shadow*, and must be contrasted, as well as compared, with that which it represents. Evidently it is used in its highest sense, signifying that Jesus Christ is "the brightness of his Father's glory, and the express image of his person"—that he possesses the same nature and perfections.

In Col. iii. 10 believers are said to have "put on the new man, which is renewed in knowledge after the image of Him that created him." The image of God into which believers are renewed consists in knowledge—not in mere intellectual knowledge, but true wisdom. Originally, God not only created man an intelligent being, but of such moral nature that he was capable of knowing, loving and serving him. Depravity—the result of the fall of man—has blinded and perverted his intellect, so that "the natural man receiveth not the things of the

Spirit of God, neither can he know them." The renewing influence of the Holy Spirit, removing the cause of blindness, enlightens the soul. With open or unveiled face it beholds the glory of God. Man was created in the image of God. He is now, by the Holy Spirit, created anew in the same image. The renewed image consists in that knowledge which a pure mind only can possess. The original image, then, must have been the same.

Again, believers, as Paul teaches, were "predestinated to be conformed to the image of his Son,"* and this is explained when the same apostle says, they were chosen before the foundation of the world, that they should be "holy and without blame before him in love."† They bear the image of Christ, and consequently the image of God, as they become holy. The image, therefore, consists in holiness. And this is in accordance with the language of the same apostle, when he

* Rom. viii. 29. † Eph. i. 4.

says of believers: "But we all, with open face beholding as in a glass the glory of the Lord, are changed into the same image from glory to glory, even as by the Spirit of the Lord."* The same truth is taught by Solomon when he says: "Lo, this only have I found, that God hath made man upright." †

The inspired account of the creation of man, then, conducts us to the undoubting conclusion that his soul is *spirit*, not *matter*. God is spirit, and it is absurd to say that matter, however refined or organized, can bear the image of spirit, especially the intellectual and moral image of spirit. God is an infinite spirit: he made man a finite spirit. He is an infinitely intelligent spirit: he made man a finitely intelligent spirit. He is infinitely and immutably holy: he made man finitely and mutably holy. Now, to say that a material organism can have the intellectual and moral image of the infinite spirit, is to say that two substances of radically different na-

* 2 Cor. iii. 18. † Eccl. vii. 29.

tures may possess the same properties or qualities, which is absurd.

We have precisely the same evidence that the soul of man is spirit as that God is spirit. For, in the first place, the same words in Hebrew and Greek are used with reference to both, viz.: RUAH and PNEUMA. The Psalmist says: "Thou sendest forth thy spirit, they are created." The Hebrew word for spirit is *ruah;* the Greek, as in the Septuagint, is *pneuma.* Speaking of the death of man, Solomon says: "The spirit returns to God who gave it." Here the same Hebrew and Greek words are used as in the preceding passage. It would be easy to give an indefinite number of similar examples. Paul brings the two together thus: "For what man knoweth the things of a man, save the spirit (*pneuma*) of man which is in him? Even so the things of God knoweth no man, but the spirit (*pneuma*) of God." *

In the second place, God is represented as,

* 1 Cor. ii. 11.

in a peculiar sense, the Father or Creator of *the spirits* of men. At death the dust returns to the earth as it was, "and the spirit shall return unto God who gave it." God is the Creator of the bodies of men, but he gives their spirits in a sense in which he does not give their bodies. He "stretcheth forth the heavens and layeth the foundation of the earth, and formeth the spirit of man within him." * The spirit is not generated, as is the body, but God forms it in man. Accordingly, the apostle reasons thus: "Furthermore, we have had fathers of our flesh which corrected us, and we gave them reverence: shall we not much rather be in subjection to the Father of spirits and live?" † On this passage McNight remarks: "By distinguishing between the fathers of our *flesh* and the Father of our *spirits*, the apostle teaches us that we derive only our flesh from our parents, but our spirit from God." "The rational soul," says Owen, "which is immediately

* Zech. xii. 1. † Heb. xii. 9.

created and infused, having *no other* father but God himself." "Father of our spirits," says Doddridge, "by whom that noble part of our nature was produced, in the production of which our earthly parents had no share."

3. In the third place, as already remarked, the soul possesses the same properties by which God is proved to be spirit, though it is finite. God is an intelligent Being, a voluntary Agent, and possesses moral character, therefore he is spirit. The soul possesses the same properties, therefore it is spirit.

But how does all this prove the immortality of the soul? It reveals the *nature* of the soul, and thus justifies, and even demands, the conclusion that it is immortal. If the soul were, like the body, *material*, the probability would seem to be that it dies when the body dies. But it is *spirit*—a substance of a radically different nature. Therefore the causes which produce the death of the material nature cannot affect the death of the spiritual nature. The soul is spirit, and, therefore, it is not, like the body, subject to decay and death. It is in the image of God, and therefore will not die. That the annihilationists see the force of this argument is evident from their efforts to prove that the image of God does not belong to the soul.

And here it may be worth while to notice their peculiar reasonings. The image of God, in which man was created, says one of them, was not "intellectual, for God is omniscient." That is to say, a finite intelligence cannot be in the image or likeness of the infinite intelligence. This is absurd, and it flatly contradicts Paul, who teaches that believers are renewed *in knowledge* after the image of Him who created man. The same writer says, the image was not "moral, for God is holy, and the attribute or characteristic of holiness presumes the possession of the knowledge of good and evil, and this knowledge man did not possess when he was made, and it was this that he was forbidden to obtain." * Strange sentiments, these! Man, we are told, could not be holy without the knowledge of good and evil, and this knowledge he was forbidden to obtain. Of course, then, he was forbidden to be holy, and would have sinned if he had become holy! Can anything be more absurd? It is not true that holiness presumes the possession of any knowledge that man was forbidden to gain. Holiness is conformity to God's law, which was written on his heart, and "love is the fulfilling of the law." Can any one believe that our first parents must sin against God before they could love and obey him? The truth is, man, as he came from the hand of God, must have been holy or unholy, for his soul possesses moral affections of which it can no more divest itself than it can revolutionize its nature; and those affections are necessarily right or wrong, holy or sinful, and so are the acts which flow from them. To say, there-

* "Quest. of Ages," p. 13.

fore, as does this writer, that, "in his primeval state," man was innocent and "very good," but not *holy*, is absurd.

Another writer of the same creed says: "The creation in the divine likeness no more proves man's absolute immortality than it proves his eternal pre-existence, his omniscience or his possession of any other divine attribute."* If by the phrase "absolute immortality" he means an immortality which is either underived or independent of God, we contend for no such immortality. But if he means immortality in the sense in which this word is universally applied to the soul, as already explained, he talks absurdly, and contradicts his own doctrine. He himself teaches that believers in Christ are to possess immortality. Does he mean by this that they are to possess one of the divine attributes? The bodies of the saints at the resurrection are to "put on immortality." Will they be clothed with divine attributes? May

* "Debt and Grace," p. 166.

not the soul of man, then, be immortal, without becoming infinite?

Another dashing writer resorts to syllogistic reasoning thus: "Formally stated, their argument is this: 1. God only hath immortality. 2. Man is created in the image of God. 3. Therefore man is immortal." And he shows up the absurdity of the argument by another syllogism: "1. God is omnipresent. 2. Man is created in the image of God. 3. Therefore man is omnipresent!"* It is scarcely necessary to say to the intelligent reader that sensible men are not accustomed to resort to such nonsense in their reasonings as this writer attributes to them. The argument, correctly stated, is this: 1. God is a spirit. 2. The soul of man was created in the image of God. 3. Therefore the soul of man is spirit. Another syllogism is necessary to complete the argument, viz.: 1. Spirit is not, like matter, subject to decay and death. 2. The soul of man is spirit. 3. Therefore the

* "Mortal and Immortal," p. 9.

soul of man is not subject to decay and death.

It may be worth while to pause here long enough to expose another piece of shallow sophistry. Replying to the argument that "the soul of man is immaterial, and therefore is immortal," one of our authors says: "The premise is merely a negative proposition, from which a positive conclusion cannot be justly drawn. It merely states what the soul of man is *not.*" And he tests the logic thus: "Man is not an ant, therefore he is an archangel. This paper is *not ivory,* therefore it *is gold.*" * This is a totally incorrect statement of the argument. The man who would reason thus would simply render himself ridiculous. There are but two substances in the universe, the material and the immaterial, or matter and spirit; and when the advocates of the immortality of the soul say that it is immaterial, they mean that it is spirit, not matter. This usage of the word

* "Quest. of Ages," p. 4.

immaterial must be known to every scholar. The proposition, therefore, is not merely a negative one: it is both negative and positive. The meaning is that the soul is not matter, but spirit, and therefore it is not mortal, but is immortal.

The inspired history of the creation of man, then, proves that his soul is spirit, not matter. And if it is spirit, it is immortal, unless spirits die.

But we are met with the triumphant reply that this argument proves all animals immortal, and, therefore, proves too much. "Are not their souls," it is asked, "reduced to nonentity by means of death?" But where is the evidence that the spirits of animals are reduced to nonentity by death? "Nor can we find anything," says Butler, "throughout the whole *analogy of nature*, to afford us even the slightest presumption that animals ever lose their living powers, much less if it were possible that they lose them by death, for we have no faculties wherewith to trace any beyond or through it, so as to see what becomes of them. This event removes them from our view. It destroys the *sensible* proof, which we had before their death, of their being possessed of living powers, but does not appear to afford the least reason to believe that they are then or by that event deprived of them." * It is neither wise nor safe to assume without evidence that the spirits of animals perish, and to conclude that, therefore, the souls of men die also.

But if there is no reason to believe that the spirits of animals perish, the evidence must be very strong that the souls of men are immortal; for they possess an incomparably higher nature, and, therefore, as we must conclude, an incomparably higher destiny. The instincts of animals do not approximate the noble intellectual powers of the soul of man; they are utterly incapable of moral character, the peculiar glory of man, or of conceiving of the eternal future, and of

* "Analogy."

being influenced by the motives drawn from the future. If, therefore, it were certain that what are called *the spirits* of animals become extinct, this would not afford even a presumptive evidence that the soul of man, created in the image of God, dies. The argument, therefore, from the creation of man, is unanswerable.

CHAPTER IV.

THE RATIONAL ARGUMENT.

IT will be satisfactory now to inquire how far the known properties of the soul confirm the obvious meaning of the Scriptures respecting its nature and destiny. Some of the annihilationist authors insist that "whatever we know of a future life must come to us by direct revelation," that "reason cannot prove man to be immortal—the oracle is dumb, or, like those of Delphi and Dodona, mutters only an ambiguous reply that leaves us in utter bewilderment." It is true that some philosophers, both in ancient and modern times, have doubted or denied the immortality of the soul, but many of them have also doubted or denied the existence of God. Now, it is certain (for the Scriptures so declare) that the works of nature afford innumerable clear proofs of his being, and illustrations of his perfections. The same modes of reasoning that led them to false conclusions on the latter subject may have misled them on the former. He who could study the wonders of nature without discovering the existence of nature's God might easily study the visible man without learning the nature and destiny of the invisible soul. On both of these subjects we doubtless need the light of revelation, but the teachings of revelation on both may be confirmed by those of reason. When we have gained, by the light of revelation, the idea of one infinitely perfect God, we can see clearly, in the works of nature, the evidences of his being and of his perfections. And so, when we have learned from the Scriptures the nature of the soul, we may discover, in its known properties, strong confirmation of their obvious teaching. For if the works of the infinite Spirit reveal his nature and attributes, it is absurd to assert that the works of finite spirits cannot do the same for them. As in studying the character of God, so in examining into the nature of the soul, we must avail ourselves of both sources of information, revelation and facts.

But another writer, of the same creed, magnifies the discoveries of the science of physiology as strongly confirming the doctrine of the Bible, as he understands it, that the soul is mortal. He talks learnedly of "the microscopic *spermatozoon* in which the man is originated, and from which he is born," and which "contains within its mysterious minuteness the vital and active immaterial principle that is essentially the future man, being the soul of the future man." He tells us, too, of "the vital seminal souls" that perish and are no more.* We are disposed to give to the science of physiology all the credit which is due to it; but when we are told that it has discovered that immaterial souls perish and are no more, we boldly deny that it has made any such discoveries.

* "Quest. of Ages," pp. 35, 36.

Its investigations are limited to that which is material, and no microscope has yet been made that can reveal the immaterial soul.

Rejecting, then, the opinion that reason can afford us no light on this subject, rejecting also the unscientific pretensions of physiologists who would push us into materialism, we proceed to the inquiry, how far the known properties of the soul afford information respecting its nature and destiny. Our examination will be brief, and not at all metaphysical or obscure.

We begin what we have to say on this subject with the truth, admitted by all, that substances are known to us only by their properties. It follows legitimately, from this truth, that different properties indicate substances as different—in other words, that substances are as different from each other as their properties. For example, the properties of light are very different from those of air, and it cannot be doubted that the two substances are in their nature as different. The same may be affirmed of an indefinite number of material substances. There are certain properties in which they all agree, and, therefore, all are called *matter*. There are other properties in which they differ, indicating as great difference in the substances.

Now, if it appear that two substances have not a single property in common, but that their properties are not only different, but opposite, the conclusion is fully warranted that the substances possess radically different natures. And this being so, to call them by the same name is to abuse language and mislead the mind. But it is a fact that mind and matter possess not a single property in common. It is a fact that the properties of these two substances are not only different, but opposite. This will be made clear by comparing, or rather contrasting, the properties of mind and those of matter.

I. One of the properties of matter is *inertness*. It cannot move itself, nor stop its motion. One of the most remarkable properties of mind is *activity*. It can no more cease to think and feel than it can cease to exist. The question has been much discussed whether the mind always thinks. Locke stands prominent amongst those who answer this question negatively. We maintain that the evidence is conclusive in favor of an affirmative answer, that the mind never ceases to think. We proceed to assign reasons in support of this view:

1. All agree that, during *waking hours*, the mind is incessantly active. We cannot, if we would, cease to think. We may choose the subject that shall occupy our thoughts, but we must think. If we do not furnish our minds with a subject, they will find one, or will wander from object to object, controlled by the laws of association, till they light on some theme that takes hold of the feelings, and there confines the thoughts. On this point there is no controversy.

2. All agree that the mind is *often* active *during sleep;* for all admit that dreams do

constantly occur—that often the mind is intensely active and the feelings greatly excited in dreams. It is, then, certain that sleep does not necessarily suspend thought, for if it did there could be no such thing as dreaming. But if sleep does not suspend thought, do we know of anything connected with sleep that does at any time suspend it? If there is anything of the kind, it is certain it operates only occasionally, not uniformly, for we do often dream. But no one pretends to have discovered any other cause of the suspension of thought in sleep. Since, then, thought is not suspended by sleep, and we know of nothing connected with sleep that does at any time suspend it, the conclusion seems clearly warranted that the mind does always think during sleep—that activity is one of its essential properties.

Locke argues that it is "hard to conceive that anything should think and not be conscious of it." But the sleeping man is conscious of thinking, although he does not always, on waking, *remember* his thoughts. But Locke replies to this: "That the soul in a sleeping man should be this moment busy a-thinking, and the next moment, in a waking man, not remember nor be able to recollect one jot of all those thoughts, is very hard to be conceived." To this we answer—

1st. That very often, during our waking hours, we entirely fail to remember the thoughts that have but just occupied our minds. Who has not often, whilst in conversation, suddenly lost the thought he was just about to express, and been wholly unable to recall it? This is very common, especially when anything has occurred suddenly to interrupt the train of thought. Is it strange, then, that on awaking from sound sleep, and finding ourselves surrounded with objects wholly different from those which have occupied the mind, we should fail to recall our sleeping thoughts, especially when there is nothing to call our attention to them? Some of our waking thoughts we wholly forget, others we remember indistinctly, whilst others are vividly impressed on our minds. The same principle governs our recollection of waking and of sleeping thoughts. That is to say, whatever takes strong hold of the feelings is remembered distinctly, whilst whatever awakens little interest is forgotten or imperfectly remembered. A distressing or a delightful dream is likely to be remembered, whilst dreams that have not strongly interested the feelings are forgotten.

Sir William Hamilton, giving his own experience, says: "I have always observed that, when suddenly awaked during sleep (and to ascertain the fact I have caused myself to be roused at different seasons of the night), I have always been able to observe that I was in the middle of a dream. The recollection of this dream was not always equally vivid. On some occasions I was able to trace it back until the train was gradually lost at a remote distance; on others I was hardly aware of more than one or two of the latter links of the chain, and sometimes was scarcely certain of more than the fact that I was not awakened from an unconscious state." The experience of Hamilton, we do not doubt, corresponds with that of most persons whose attention has been turned to this point. It certainly corresponds with our own experience through a series of years; and we fully endorse the following statement made by him: "I have myself at different times turned my attention to the point, and, as far as my observations go, they certainly tend to prove that, during sleep, the mind is never either inactive or wholly unconscious of its activity."

2d. But that the activity of the mind during sleep is not disproved by the fact that often persons do not remember to have dreamed, is fully established by the phenomena of *somnambulism*. That in this state the mind is active, often intensely active, cannot be doubted; and yet the somnambulist, when awake, never remembers what he was thinking of when asleep. "It is the peculiarity of somnambulism—it is the differential quality by which that state is contradistinguished from the state of dreaming—that we have no recollection, when we awake, of what has occurred during its continuance. Consciousness is thus cut in two: memory does not connect the train of consciousness in the one state with the train of consciousness in the other. When the patient again relapses into the state of somnambulism, he again remembers all that had occurred during every former alternative of that state. But he not only remembers this: he recalls also the events of his normal existence, so that, whereas the patient in his somnambulic crisis has a memory of his whole life, in his waking intervals he has a memory only of half of his life."* It is not only true that in the somnambulic state the mind is active, but it possesses an extraordinary activity. "In this remarkable state," says Hamilton, "the various mental faculties are usually in a higher

* Hamilton.

degree of power than in the natural;" and he mentions having three works written during the crisis by three different somnambulists. It is, then, clear beyond a question that the mind is often intensely active in sleep, whilst it has no recollection in its waking hours of the thoughts that have occupied it.

3. There are facts which demonstrate that even in what is called the *comatose state* the mind is active. We are aware that this has been denied. Dr. Good, in his "Book of Nature," maintains that in complete paroxysms of apoplexy, sleepy coma, suspended animation from drowning, and the like, no man is conscious of a single thought or idea. But even if we had no facts to prove the contrary, all that could be affirmed would be that, on coming out of these states, persons do not *remember* to have been thinking. But Dr. Abercrombie states the following interesting fact: "A case has been related to me of a boy who at the age of four received a fracture of the skull, for which he underwent the operation

of trepan. He was at the time in a state of perfect stupor, and after his recovery retained no recollection either of the accident or the operation. At the age of fifteen, during the delirium of a fever, he gave his mother a correct description of the operation and the persons who were present at it, with their dress and other minute particulars. He had never been observed to allude to it before, and no means were known by which he could have acquired the circumstances which he mentioned."* He mentions several other facts proving the activity of the mind in perfect apoplexy.

The evidence seems conclusive that the mind always thinks—that activity is an essential property of mind. It follows that the mind is not matter, but a substance of an opposite nature.

This conclusion is greatly strengthened by the fact that the activity of the mind is *voluntary*. Whilst we cannot cease thinking, we

* "Intellec. Philos.," Part iii., Sec. 3, 4.

are yet conscious of the power to give direction to our thoughts—to choose the subject about which our thoughts at any particular time shall be occupied. In proof of this we need only appeal to the consciousness of every man. Now, it is certain that matter is governed by fixed laws. Voluntariness, therefore, cannot be predicated of it. Were the mind material, it must act as it is acted on. The certain fact that its activity, so far as the subject of its thoughts is concerned, is voluntary, proves that it is not matter.

The argument is complete when we state the further fact that much of the activity of the mind is not only voluntary, but *moral.* That the human mind has thoughts, feelings and purposes which may be properly characterized as *right* or *wrong,* is a truth which is intuitive. Few comparatively have ever denied it even in theory. All have acknowledged it in practice. But were the mind a material organism governed by fixed laws, its acts would be neither right nor wrong.

Men would be incapable alike of virtue or vice.

II. The mind presents as strong a contrast with matter in its other properties as in its ceaseless, voluntary, moral activity. Matter, for example, is *extended*, mind is not. Matter is *divisible*, mind is *indivisible*. Matter possesses the property of *attraction*, mind does not. As already remarked, these two substances, mind and matter, possess not a single property in common. In all their properties they stand in striking contrast. The conclusion is fully warranted that the mind is not material.

III. It is important to notice another remarkable feature of the soul which may reveal its nature, viz.: its capacity to look to the future, and its susceptibility of being influenced by motives drawn from the eternal future, together with its intense desire to live for ever. From early childhood it begins to look forward, and to have desires, hopes and fears respecting future interests. Nor is it possible to confine such thoughts and anxieties to the boundaries of time. Under the impulse of its nature, the soul overleaps those boundaries, and inquires anxiously respecting the eternal ages, and both its moral conduct and its happiness are mightily influenced by the prospects that open before it along the track of those ages. Hope seizes upon and rejoices exceedingly in a bright future, and fears agitate the soul when the future is overcast with dark and portentous clouds. Nothing short of eternal life can satisfy its hopes or subdue its fears. All but the most degraded men act habitually more or less under the influence of motives drawn from eternity. Their moral conduct is more or less controlled by such motives, and their happiness is increased or diminished by hope or fear.

Such, in a few words, are the leading features of the human soul. Others might be mentioned, but these are sufficient for the argument. In view of these properties of the soul, we raise two questions, viz.: first, To what conclusion do they conduct us respecting its *nature?* and, secondly, To what conclusion do they conduct us respecting its *destiny?*

1. What is the *nature* of the soul, as discovered through its properties? Is it *matter*, or is it *spirit?* It is certainly the one or the other, since these are the only substances known to men. One of the annihilationist writers, as already quoted, once and again objects to what he calls "the silent assumption that because the soul of man is *not matter*, therefore *it is spirit;*" and he evidently seeks to make the impression that it is neither matter nor spirit. And yet he applies to the whole man, soul and body, the language, "Dust thou art, and unto dust shalt thou return." But it is certain that the soul is a *substance*, for it has *properties*, and until some third substance shall be discovered, we must conclude that it is either matter or spirit He affirms, indeed, that

"mere human reason does not and cannot know anything of *spirit*, except as apprehending the existence and ubiquity of God through a consideration of his visible works."* This is a mere assertion, and it is absurd. The works of the infinite Spirit reveal him: why may not the works of finite spirits reveal them? The truth is, we are quite as well acquainted with spirit as with matter. We know nothing of either except what we learn from their properties, but we are as well acquainted with the properties of spirit as with those of matter.

We have before us, then, two substances whose properties are essentially different, and even opposite. The one is inert, the other is active. The one moves only as it is moved, the other is perpetually moving itself. The one is controlled by fixed laws, the other is constantly putting forth voluntary acts. The one, because governed by fixed laws, is incapable of moral and accountable action, the

* "Quest. of Ages," pp. 5, 34.

other is a moral agent, the subject of a moral government. Now, the conclusion to which we are authorized, and even constrained, to come, is this: Since these substances are known to us only by their properties, and since their properties are essentially different, and even opposite, the substances are in their nature essentially different. The one we call *matter*, the other we call *spirit*. But it matters little by what names they may be designated: the radical difference in their natures is demonstrated. And yet, as before remarked, it is impossible for any one to tell what *spirit* is, except by saying it is a substance that thinks, reasons, chooses, loves, hates, rejoices, sorrows, hopes, fears. It is enough, however, that the two substances differ essentially in their nature.

2. The next question relates to the *destiny* of the soul. To what conclusion are we conducted respecting its destiny by the consideration of its properties? 1st. In the first place, since it is certain that it is a substance whose

nature is radically different from that of the body, there is no reason to suppose that the death of the body destroys or impairs its life. For since the two substances are in nature radically different, they must be operated on by causes as different. Those causes, therefore, which destroy the life of the body, such as a bullet passing into the head or the heart, in all probability have no effect whatever upon the soul, except to dissolve the mysterious tie that binds the two together. Since, then, there is no reason to think that the death of the body impairs the life of the soul, and since we know of no other causes which are likely to operate on the soul to extinguish its life, the only conclusion to which we can come is, that it survives the body, and lives in another state. Still further, since we know the soul only as an active, thinking substance, since activity seems to belong to its very nature, it cannot be supposed that at the death of the body it ceases to be active and becomes unconscious. 2d. The innate desire of the soul for immortality, together with its capacity to conceive the eternal future, and to be mightily influenced, both in its moral conduct and its happiness, by considerations and motives drawn from eternity, indicate the purpose of the Creator that it shall live for ever. But it is objected that this argument "is based upon the assumption that an ardent desire to possess an object is an evidence that the object so ardently desired is actually possessed," and that "if, as an argument, it were logical and sound, it would fill the face of the inhabited earth with wealthy and powerful men, for every man who has an ardent desire for money would be a millionaire, and every man who thirsts for power would be a potentate." * This objection would be a complete refutation of the argument if we were weak enough to contend that the mere fact that men desire immortality proves them immortal. But this is not the argument. The argument is based on the broad principle that the de-

* "Quest. of Ages," p. 9; 10.

sires, capacities and susceptibilities which God has imparted to his creatures were designed to adapt them to the spheres in which they were to act, and to the destinies they were to fill; and consequently those desires, capacities and susceptibilities do reveal the purposes of God respecting them. This principle is seen to prevail throughout the whole animal kingdom. This will not be disputed. But let us see how the principle applies to man. His Creator gave him appetites, and he provided the proper means for their use and gratification. He endowed him with natural and social affections, and thus his purpose was indicated that men should live in families and in society. He imparted to the soul a taste for the beautiful, and he filled the visible universe with beautiful objects. He gave to the soul a moral sense, and he gave the moral law to guide it. He imparted to it moral affections, and he bade it love him and its fellow-creatures, and be happy. Thus far it is certain that for every appetite, affection, taste and susceptibility of man God provided corresponding spheres of action and means of gratification, and those appetites, affections, tastes and susceptibilities indicate his purposes concerning man.

But the Creator also gave to the soul such a nature that it is capable of looking to the eternal future, and of being powerfully influenced by motives drawn thence, and that it intensely desires to live for ever. And here a broad distinction is to be made between those desires which belong to the nature of the soul as it came from the hand of God, and those which result from ignorance and depravity. The former clearly indicate the purposes of the Creator respecting the soul; the latter are the evidences of its estrangement from him. "The love of money is the root of all evil." Will it be pretended that God originally planted this root in the soul? The love of power is selfishness. Will it be said that this is native to the soul as it came from the hand of the Creator? Is it not written "that God hath made man upright"? And is it not true that the wiser and the more virtuous men become, the less they thirst for either riches or power?

But how is it with the desire for immortality? Is it, like the love of money and of power, the result of depravity and alienation from God? It exists in all men, nor is it possible for any one, if he would, to banish it from his soul. Depravity may weaken but cannot destroy it. And it is certain that the wiser and the holier men become, the stronger grows this desire to live for ever. It is the wicked and degraded who say, "Let us eat and drink, for to-morrow we die." It is the wise and good who live and labor "in hope of eternal life." Moreover, this is a feature of the soul to which the Scriptures constantly appeal. "What will it profit a man," asks our Lord, "if he shall gain the whole world and lose his soul?" The attempt to place such a desire on an equality with the sinful love of money or of power shows how loosely some of those men reason.

But the argument is still stronger. It is not based on even an intense desire which belongs to the nature of the soul, but also on a corresponding capacity and susceptibility. The soul is capable of conceiving of the eternal future, and it is susceptible of feeling powerfully the motives drawn from that future. Its moral conduct and its happiness are thus powerfully influenced. It is so constituted that it cannot even enjoy present blessings unless the future seem bright. Hope must sweeten the blessings we now possess, or fear will embitter them. Hope must lighten present trials, or fear will add to their weight.

Now, will any one pretend that these noble features of the soul give no indications of the purposes of the Creator respecting it? Are these to constitute the one fearful exception to the general rule that for every capacity, susceptibility and desire which the Creator imparted to man he provided a corresponding sphere of action and means of gratification? If these do not constitute a marvelous exception, then it is certain that the innate desire of the soul to live for ever, taken in connection with its capacity to feel the motives drawn from eternity, indicates the purpose of the Creator that it should possess immortality. Otherwise we must conclude that he designed men to live under a delusive hope of eternal life, or that he so formed the soul that, knowing the truth, it must be wretched. Most assuredly the features of the soul now under consideration reveal the design of the Creator that it should live for ever; and if such was his purpose, beyond a question he imparted to it a nature adapted to its destiny. It is therefore immortal.

IV. These arguments are greatly strengthened by the almost universal belief in the doctrine of the soul's immortality in all ages and nations. We are aware that the fact of this general belief has been called in question.

But with the exception of some of those called philosophers, there is no ground for doubt on the subject. Archbishop Whateley, whilst insisting that the doctrine of immortality was not really known till Jesus Christ revealed it, acknowledges that the ancient heathen lawgivers taught it "from a persuasion of its importance for men's conduct."* And it is certain that it has entered into all the different forms of religion. Many of the gods worshiped by the ancient pagan nations, it is known, were deceased men. "As soon," says Gibbon, "as it was allowed that sages and heroes who had lived or who had died for the benefit of their country were exalted to a state of power and immortality, it was universally confessed that they deserved, if not the adoration, at least the reverence, of all mankind."† The learned Dr. Leland speaks of this form of idolatry as one which began very early and prevailed very gener-

* "Future State," p. 24.

† Gibbon's "Decline and Fall of Rome," v. i., p. 18.

ally in the world, and "which produced an amazing multiplicity of gods, and continually increased." He quotes the statement of Philo Biblius that "the most ancient barbarians, especially the Phœnicians and Egyptians, from whom other people took this custom, reckoned those amongst the greatest gods who had been the inventors of things useful and necessary to human life, and who had been benefactors to the nations." Cicero said that "almost the whole heaven is filled with the human race; that upon searching into the ancient accounts, and what the Greek writers have deduced from them, it will be found that even those that are accounted the greater deities, *dii majorum gentium,* were taken from among men into heaven, that their sepulchres were shown in Greece." *

The practice of necromancy, which prevailed in the days of Moses, proves the same thing, for "it is the art of raising up the ghosts of deceased persons to get informa-

* Leland "On Revolution," v. i., pp. 99, 104.

tion from them concerning future events." The ancient doctrine of metempsychosis could not have existed without the doctrine of the immortality of the soul. "The Egyptians believed that at the death of men their souls transmigrated into other human bodies, and that if they had been vicious they were imprisoned in the bodies of unclean or ill-conditioned beasts, to expiate in them their past transgressions, and that after a revolution of some centuries they again animated other human bodies."* In one form or another the doctrine of the soul's immortality has been almost universal, and, as Dr. Isaac Watts well remarks: "The doctrine of rewards and punishments in a separate state of souls hath been one of the very chief principles or motives whereby virtue and religion have been maintained in this sinful world throughout all former ages and nations."

Very few indeed of all the unnumbered millions who have believed this doctrine

* Rollin's "Ancient History," v. i., p. 114.

could have given any philosophical reasons in favor of its truth, much less could they have given any satisfactory account of the state of the soul after death. Some, too, have attempted to prove it by arguments which are not sound. The same may be said of the universal belief in the being of God. The prevalence of this latter belief is accounted for by referring it to man's moral nature. The mind is so constituted that it must and will have religion of some kind, and, therefore, men will have some object of religious worship. May not the general belief of mankind in the doctrine of the immortality of the soul be accounted for in the same way? Can it be accounted for in any other way?

It is a remarkable fact that skeptical philosophers, with all their learning, have been wholly unable to shake the faith of any considerable portion of our race in either of these great doctrines for any considerable length of time. The French philosophers might deify Reason, and inscribe on the public cemeteries, "Death is an eternal sleep;" but the deep innate convictions of the outraged human soul soon made their voice heard above the tumult of passion and crime, reasserted the being of God, and at the same time wiped out the degrading inscription from the cemeteries. A French atheist on trial for his life might say, "My name is Danton—my abode will soon be nonentity," * but the shudder with which the sentiment is heard is the soul's protest against the degrading doctrine. The fact that the faith of the great majority of mankind in the immortality of the soul, like that in the being of a God, however mixed up with superstitions and absurdities, has remained firm throughout all ages, affords strong evidence that it finds its foundation in the very nature of man, and if so, it must be true. Had it been a doctrine of philosophers, it would have been received, like their other doctrines, by but a small por-

* Allison's "History of Europe," p. 36.

tion of the race. Had it been merely traditionary, it would never have taken such hold of the human mind. To overcome this deep-seated conviction of the soul is a Herculean task. They who contend against the noblest convictions and aspirations of man should be cogent reasoners; and the proof must indeed be conclusive which would justify us in renouncing a faith apparently grounded in the nature of the soul.

CHAPTER V.

THE INTERMEDIATE STATE.

WE come now to the third question proposed for discussion, viz.: WHAT DO THE SCRIPTURES TEACH RESPECTING THE STATE OF THE SOUL BETWEEN DEATH AND THE RESURRECTION?

Man is a fallen creature. By his transgression he has incurred the penalty of God's law. It is important, in the further discussion of this subject, to inquire whether the penalty denounced against sin has deprived the soul of its immortality. Or do the teachings of the Scriptures respecting the intermediate state lead to the conclusion, that the soul dies with the body, and that between death and the resurrection man has no conscious existence? The sentence pronounced upon Adam (Gen. iii. 14–19) is interpreted by annihilationists to mean that man is wholly of earthly origin, and at death is reduced to "elemental atoms;" that "no part of man remains in a separate conscious state in death, but that the whole man lies in unconsciousness till called to new life by the resurrection;" that "death is a state of non-existence."

Hudson, shrinking from the absurdities of materialism, to which his theory inevitably leads, and holding that the soul continues to exist as "an entity," regards it as dependent upon the physical organism for active existence. He thinks it necessary to teach that it has, in the intermediate state, a kind of half consciousness, a degree or so above annihilation. "May we not suppose," he asks, "that in the disembodied state the soul is lost in an intuition of its past history, with no process of thinking, and with no note of time? Not a state of thinking—perhaps, on the other hand, not of unconsciousness—but of momentary all-consciousness, the same to those who die soon or late, the resurrection and the judgment close following." And he consoles himself and his readers with the suggestion: "May not a little repose be better for us ere the dawn of the sleepless, endless day?" * Grave as the subject is, there is something in this query so ludicrous as to provoke a smile. The soul, we are apt to think, must have become greatly exhausted in its few years of thought and labor here, to require a few hundred years of repose before it is prepared to enter upon its eternal rest! As for the supposed state of the soul, in which it does not think, yet is not unconscious, possesses all-consciousness and is lost in the intuition of its past history, it is no conceivable state at all. The sentences just quoted are simply a string of words conveying no idea, but poorly concealing the degrading doctrine which the writer dare not plainly advocate. If it be found, on examination, that the Scriptures teach that the soul survives the body and passes into another state of con-

* "Debt and Grace," pp. 260, 261.

scious existence, a very strong evidence will thus be obtained in favor of its immortality.

1. Here it is important to say that nothing that we know of the nature and properties of the soul affords the slightest evidence that it is dependent upon the body for conscious, active existence. So long as it continues in the body, its activities must be exerted mainly through the body; but whilst we have no means of knowing how it will put forth its activities in its disembodied state, we certainly have no reason to believe that it cannot act in such a state. On the contrary, it may be capable of higher activities than whilst in the gross, material body.

II. Still further, it is a fact of great significance that nothing is more familiar to the mind of the reader of the Scriptures than the activities of spirits. Angels, it is true, have sometimes appeared in human forms, as when they appeared to Abraham and Lot. But we are expressly taught that angels are "spirits," and we constantly read in the New

Testament of "unclean spirits." Dr. Morris, one of the annihilationist authors, says of the devil and his angels, "These wicked spirits are in the heavenlies as in their province, the possession and occupancy of which they are yet permitted of God to retain." And he gives us an alarming idea of the activities and powers of the prince of evil spirits. He says: "As men in general have little or no conception of the moral power of Satan for evil, so have they no adequate conception of his intellectual and physical power for mischief on the earth. . . . He is independent of all mechanical contrivances and chemical appliances. . . . And by his own mere mental confidence, whenever God permits him, Satan can subordinate the laws and apply the forces of electricity and meteorology, and can change the condition of animal chemistry, and can cause muscular contraction," etc. He extols "Satan's proficiency in mental and moral science," as evinced in the experimental history of the saints of God, in all the temptations which they endure. He tells us: "There is no reason for believing that the presence of demons in the midst of human society is more restricted, or that their evil power is less active, now than in the days of the Son of man and of his apostles. . . . Men have little or no conception of the intelligence and power of demons, who can not only afflict and torture men through the corporeal organism, but can form a superhuman and spiritual *amalgam* (so to speak) with the souls of men. They *are spirits, evil spirits*, and seven of them, yea, many of them, can thus combine with one human soul," * etc.

It is, then, admitted that one of the most familiar truths in the Scriptures is the existence, the immense activity and power of *spirits*. But if angels and evil spirits not only possess a conscious existence, but put forth incessant activities without material bodies, if they can act either through the human body or without any body, there

* "Quest. of Ages," pp. 70–73.

can be nothing improbable in the doctrine that the spirits of men, good and bad, when released from their bodies, will be equally active. Nay, the fact that disembodied spirits do live and act compels the conclusion, unless there be positive evidence to the contrary, that the spirits of men will also live and act out of the body. Accordingly, the inspired writers speak as familiarly of being out of the body as of being in it, of being absent from the body as of being present in it, of putting off their tabernacle, the body, as of putting off their garments.

III. The doctrine that the soul survives the body and possesses a conscious existence, happy or unhappy, between death and the resurrection, is clearly established, as we believe, by a comparison of the different classes of passages in the Scriptures bearing on this point. We have no hesitation in admitting that there are many passages which, if they are to be taken as teaching *all* that is true of the nature and destiny of man, do support the doctrine that the soul as well as the body dies. Nay, they teach more than this, viz.: that death is the final end of man, and that he is to have no future. Besides the sentence pronounced on Adam (Gen. iii. 19), such passages as the following are adduced as proving that the soul dies with the body: "For in death there is no remembrance of thee: in the grave who shall give thee thanks?" "Wilt thou show wonders to the dead? shall the dead arise and praise thee?" "The dead praise not the Lord, neither any that go down into silence." "Put not your trust in princes, nor in the son of man, in whom there is no help. His breath goeth forth, he returneth to his earth, in that very day his thoughts perish." "For the living know that they shall die, but the dead know not anything, neither have they any more a reward; for the memory of them is forgotten." "For the grave cannot praise thee, death cannot celebrate thee: they that go down into the pit cannot hope for thy truth. The living, the living, he shall praise thee as I do this day." "If I wait, the grave is mine house. I have made my bed in the darkness. I have said to corruption, Thou art my father; to the worm, Thou art my mother and my sister. And where now is my hope? as for my hope, who shall see it?" *

It is readily admitted that these passages favor the doctrine they are cited to prove, if they reveal all that is true of the state of the dead; but, as just remarked, it must also be noted that some of them, thus understood, prove a great deal more than the annihilationists believe. They prove that death is the final end of man's being—it is his utter destruction. Take, for example, the language of Job: "The grave is mine house," *i. e.*, my final abode. "I have said to corruption, Thou art my father; to the worm, Thou art my mother and my sister," *i. e.*, I have no

* Ps. vi. 5; Ps. xxxviii. 10; Ps. cxv. 17; Ps. cxlvi. 3, 4; Eccles. ix. 5, 6, 10; Isa. xxxviii. 18, 19; Job xvii. 13, 15.

more a future to hope for than corruption and the worm. "And where now is my hope?" The language, taken by itself, expresses in the strongest manner the dying out of hope—the blasting of all prospects for the future. Is this, it may be asked, the language of one who has the hope of a glorious resurrection and of eternal bliss? And why all this gloomy talk about corruption and the worm, when, as the annihilationists insist, the resurrection will appear to be but a moment after death?—when, as they say, Paul desired to die because he would *seem* to be with Christ immediately?* In not one of these passages is there the slightest intimation that there is to be a resurrection, or that man has a future to hope for. Why, then, do not the advocates of the mortality of the soul go farther, and infer from these passages that death is the end of man? Do they not insist that death is the final extinction of the beasts, and does not Solomon put man on a level

* "Debt and Grace," pp. 260, 261.

with the beasts? "For that which befalleth the sons of men befalleth beasts; even one thing befalleth them: as one dieth, so dieth the other; yea, they have all one breath, so that a man hath no pre-eminence above a beast; for all is vanity."* How, then, do these men escape the conclusion that death is the end of man?—that there is for him no eternal future? They must take the ground that these passages do not teach *the whole truth respecting man*—that we cannot conclude from them that man finally perishes in the grave—since there are other portions of Scripture which teach the doctrine of the resurrection. And this is the true ground. It is absurd to attempt to determine the nature of the destiny of man from any one text or any one class of texts. If we would learn the truth concerning the nature of man and concerning his destiny, we must collect all that the Scriptures say of him. The inspired writers sometimes dwell upon the frailty, the vanity, the worthlessness

* Eccles. iii. 19.

of man, as when he is compared to grasshoppers and worms. At other times they magnify his importance and dignity as bearing the image of God—as being "the image and glory of God." At one time they contemplate the death of man as the termination of all his thoughts, plans and hopes, and their minds dwell upon the silence and the darkness of the grave. At another they fix their attention upon the soul, its high destiny and its glorious or awful future, and then they tell us distinctly that when the dust returns to the earth as it was, the spirit returns to God who gave it—that the dead who have died in the Lord are now blessed, resting from their labors. The truth respecting man is to be learned from all these classes of texts, not from any one of them alone.

It is in this way we become acquainted with the character of Christ, and it is by adopting the course pursued by annihilationists that Unitarians prove him to be a creature. Is he not again and again called a man, a man of sorrows, the Son of man? Does he not say expressly, "My Father is greater than I"? Let us take such texts as these as teaching the whole truth respecting the character of Christ, and we prove him a mere man. But we say to Unitarians: These passages, it is true, teach that Christ is a man, and that there is a sense in which the Father is greater than he, but there are other passages in which he is declared to be God—to be equal with God. There must, therefore, be a sense in which he is truly God as well as a sense in which he is truly man. The only legitimate conclusion from a comparison of all the texts is that he possesses two natures, human and divine, and that, viewed as man, he is inferior to the Father, viewed as God, he is equal with the Father.

Precisely thus we ascertain what is the nature and what the destiny of man. We read that he is dust, and at death returns to dust. We also read that he has a spirit which is not dust, and does not return to the earth. We read that he sleeps all unconscious in the grave. We also read that when the body is killed or dies the soul is not killed, but still lives. We read of men dying, and being buried, and seeing corruption. We also read that at death they are absent from the body, and, if righteous, are present with the Lord. Now, we know that what each of these passages teaches is true, and we know that they do not contradict each other. How shall we reconcile them? Simply by noticing the plain fact that one class of texts speak of the present life, its works, hopes, sorrows and joys; another class speak of the future life. One class of texts have reference to man's *material* nature and its destiny; the other, to his *spiritual* nature and its destiny.

And this method of interpretation is in accordance with universal usage. The most earnest advocates of the immortality of the soul say of a man, He died and was buried, and yet they do not believe the soul died or was buried. All persons say a man was wounded and a man was grieved. No one misunderstands such language. All understand that it is the body that was wounded, the soul that grieved. Believers in the immortality of the soul have never hesitated to say that man is mortal, and that man is immortal. Man is a complex being. His two natures possess opposite qualities, and consequently opposite things are affirmed of them. He now lives in one state, he is destined soon to live in another; and widely different affirmations are made respecting these widely different states.

Let us now try to determine, by a candid comparison of the different classes of Scripture passages which treat of the nature and destiny of fallen man, whether the sentence of death pronounced on Adam doomed his soul and the souls of his posterity to a state of unconsciousness at the death of the body, or whether the Scriptures teach that the soul has a conscious existence between death and the resurrection.

1. Happily we have an inspired explanation of that sentence. Solomon has told us what takes place at death. "Then shall the dust return to the earth as it was, and the spirit shall return unto God who gave it." * From this inspired statement we learn two most important truths:

1st. That man is not wholly from the dust, that only one of his natures is derived from the earth, the other, directly from God. At death the dust—that part of man which was taken from the ground—returns to the earth as it was; but the spirit—the soul—not being from the dust, does not go to the earth, but returns to God, by whom it was given. How completely Solomon's explanation of death annihilates the learned criticisms on the Hebrew "GAH-PHAR—*elemental atoms*," by which the attempt is made to prove that man, body and soul, is formed of the dust

* Eccles. xii. 7.

and must again become dust! Solomon teaches us that man has two natures, is composed of two different substances, *matter* and *spirit.*

2d. The second truth taught in the passage under consideration is, that death does not take both body and soul into the grave, but only severs the mysterious tie which has bound them together, that the spirit, the soul, may return to God, to give account of the deeds done in the body. It is absolutely certain, therefore, that the soul, instead of sleeping in unconsciousness in the grave, passes into another state of conscious existence.

The obvious meaning of this Scripture is evaded, however, by making the Hebrew word translated *spirit* signify *breath.* Says one of our authors: "If this breath, as drawn from the surrounding atmosphere, may be said to come from God or be given by God, with the same propriety may it be said, when it leaves the body at death, to return to him."* It almost seems like trifling to expose such a criticism. Three considerations will show the absurdity of it. The first is, that the word translated *spirit* (*ruah*) is the Hebrew word constantly used to signify the Spirit of God and the spirit of man. It is, therefore, the very word which Solomon, speaking of the soul *as spirit*, would employ. Secondly, in no part of the Scriptures do we find the *body* of man placed in contrast with his *breath*. This writer, who abounds, on other occasions, in references to what he considers parallel passages, attempts no such reference here. Thirdly, in what possible sense can it be said that the *last* breath of a dying man returns to God any more than any other breath he ever drew? But language in the hands of such critics means just what they choose to make it mean.

Another writer of the same creed declines to say that in this instance the word *ruah* means *breath*, but he thinks "it may be used

* "Mortal or Immortal," pp. 40, 41.

to signify the *motion* of the soul in passing away, and passing into the custody of God." To sustain this singular notion, he gives us a curious criticism. The Hebrew word *ruah*, and the corresponding Greek word *pneuma*, he informs us, mean *spirit* when applied to God, and also to those born of God. "But to man as man the word 'spirit,' in every department of Holy Scripture, is used adjectively, as signifying only the motions and emotions of the soul."* This assertion is made for the purpose of escaping the truth that the human soul is *spirit.* It would certainly have been expedient to accompany a statement so extraordinary and so important with some sort of proof, but nothing of the kind is attempted. The statement is untrue, and is absurd. In Numbers xvi. 22, Moses and Aaron are said to have prayed thus: "O God, the God of the spirits of all flesh," etc. What sense would the language make if we should understand the word

* "Quest. of Ages," pp. 18, 19.

spirits here to mean "the motions and emotions" of all flesh? Zechariah speaks of God as Him that "formeth the spirit of man within him."* Shall we read the passage thus: "That formeth 'the motions and emotions' of man within him"? And in the passage under examination, if the word *ruah* means *motion*, what word in the sentence expresses the thing that moves?

There is no mistaking the real meaning of the passage. Man, it teaches us, is a complex being. His body is formed from the earth, and at death the *dust*—the material organism—returns to the earth as it was. But his soul is not formed of dust—it is not matter, but spirit—and, therefore, it does not go to the earth, but to God who gave it. The soul, consequently, survives the body, and is introduced by death into another state of conscious existence.

2. Our Saviour taught the same doctrine in language too clear to be misunderstood;

* Zech. xii. 1.

when sending forth his disciples on their perilous mission, he said to them: "Fear not them which kill the body, but are not able to kill the soul." * The doctrine we are opposing is that the soul dies with the body, being incapable of a conscious existence without it. If this be true, it is certain that he who kills the body does by that very act kill the soul also. He kills the soul as truly as he kills the body. But our Lord teaches that, although men may kill the body, they cannot kill the soul. It is therefore certain that the soul survives the body: death merely severs the tie that binds soul and body together, and the soul still lives.

Here, again, we have the usual resort to unsound criticism. "We must take into consideration," says one writer, "that the word here rendered *soul* is *pseuchē*, a word forty times rendered *life* in the New Testament." † And so he would translate it here. The pas-

* Matt. x. 28.

† "Mortal or Immortal," pp. 41, 42.

sage would then read thus: "Fear not them which kill the body, but are not able to kill the *life*." This sounds strangely. To kill is to destroy life, and how the *body* could be killed and the *life* remain unharmed is not quite clear, to say nothing of the very extraordinary phrase, *to kill life*. But our author interprets the passage thus: "We are not to fear them which can kill the body, or can deprive us of our brief space of life here, but cannot touch that life which is hid with Christ in God which will be bestowed upon us when our great Lifegiver shall appear"—that is, at the resurrection. According to this interpretation, the word *body* signifies "our brief space of life here"—a very extraordinary meaning certainly—and the word *life* or *soul* signifies the life which the body or person will have when raised from the dead at a future period—also a most extraordinary meaning. He refers, in justification of his most extraordinary criticism, to Matt. x. 39: "He that findeth his life shall lose it; and he that loseth his life for my sake shall find it." But here the antithesis is between *life* and *life*, making it obvious that the present life is meant in the one case and the future life in the other. But in the passage before us the antithesis is not between life and life, but between *soul* and *body*. This manifestly incorrect interpretation is exposed by another writer of the same faith thus: "And Christ speaks of man as able to kill the body, but not the soul (Matt. x. 28; Luke xii. 5), where the use of the word *life* instead of *soul* explains nothing, for in the death of the body the life is, in fact, destroyed. Nor will it meet the difficulty to say that man can destroy the life only temporarily, while God can destroy it eternally, for the same is true of the body, and the words of Christ make the distinction, not between the temporary and the eternal, but between the body and the soul. Nor can the word here rendered *soul* be taken as referring to the future, eternal life of the believer, as when it is said that his 'life is hid with Christ in God,' for this sense of the word *life* is altogether different, as the *fact* of life and the *principle* of life are different ideas,"* etc.

It is certain, then, that the soul does not die with the body, but continues to live. It is not unconscious between death and the resurrection. It lives in a happy or an unhappy state.

3. It is certain that the Apostle Paul believed that the soul may live out of the body. Speaking of the wonderful revelations vouchsafed to him, he says: "I knew a man in Christ above fourteen years ago (whether in the body, I cannot tell; whether out of the body, I cannot tell: God knoweth); such a one caught up to the third heaven. And I knew such a man (whether in the body or out of the body, I cannot tell: God knoweth), how that he was caught up into Paradise, and heard unspeakable words which it is not lawful for a man to utter."† Paul knew

* "Debt and Grace," p. 252. † 2 Cor. xii. 2, 3.

that he had been caught up to heaven, where he heard unspeakable words, but he did not know whether he was taken up soul and body, or whether his soul was, for the time, separated from the body. Now, if he had believed, with the annihilationists, that the soul can have no conscious existence out of the body, he could have had no doubt on the subject. It is certain, therefore, that he was a believer in the immortality of the soul.

But it is objected that, according to this view, Paul must have died and had a *resurrection*. Suppose it was so: did not Lazarus die and rise again? But it cannot be proved that the soul may not be separated from the body temporarily without the extinction of the natural life. The objection, then, is without force. We are told, indeed, that "all the apostle means by the phrase 'out of the body' is merely to be in vision," * but such an assertion, made in utter disregard of the language of the apostle, is worthy of notice only

* "Mortal or Immortal," p. 62.

as it shows how glaringly the Scriptures must be perverted in the advocacy of the doctrine of the mortality of the soul. Others had visions, but were never said to be *out of the body.*

4. Whilst the doctrine is taught, with entire clearness, that the souls of all men live after the death of their bodies, the state of the righteous after death is more frequently brought to view. We propose now to examine what we find in the New Testament on this point.

1st. Three of the evangelists record the appearance of Moses and Elias on the Mount of Transfiguration with our Lord. Luke records it thus: "And behold, there talked with him two men, which were Moses and Elias, who appeared in glory, and spake of his decease, which he should accomplish at Jerusalem."* Neither of the narratives leaves any ground to doubt the actual presence of those two servants of God in the mount.

* Luke ix. 30, 31

Elias was translated, body and soul, to heaven, but Moses died and his body was buried, yet the appearance of both is recorded, as if there were nothing more remarkable in the one case than in the other. It is clear, then, that Moses lived in heaven after the death of his body. Dr. Clarke, it is true, expressed the opinion that "the body of Moses was probably *raised* again as a pledge of the resurrection," but since there is not a word in the Bible countenancing the idea, it cannot be probable. There is really no more difficulty about the appearance of Moses than about the appearance of angels, of which we so often read in both the Old and New Testaments; for the angels are "all ministering spirits," as the saints are "the spirits of just men made perfect."

2d. The answer of our Lord to the prayer of the dying thief establishes the same doctrine. "Lord, remember me," he prayed, "when thou comest into thy kingdom." The answer was: "Verily I say unto thee,

To-day shalt thou be with me in Paradise." * We need not stop to inquire whether in this passage Paradise means heaven. It was certainly a place of happiness, and to that place the soul of the dying thief was to go immediately after death. His body died, and his soul entered Paradise. But there is a difficulty, we are told, "that lies like a mountain barrier" in the way of this understanding of our Saviour's language, viz.: that he said, three days after he made this promise, that he had not yet ascended to the Father. John xx. 17. This difficulty wholly disappears when we remember that, although the human nature of Christ is finite, and might not have ascended to heaven on that day, yet his divine nature is infinite, and was in heaven. There is no more difficulty, even supposing the objector rightly understands John xx. 17, than there is in the language of our Lord in John iii. 13: "And no man hath ascended up to heaven, but he that came down from heaven,

* Luke xxiii. 43.

even the Son of man, which *is* in heaven." He here claims to be at the same moment both on earth and in heaven.

An attempt is made to evade the force of the argument by a change in the punctuation, so as to make our Saviour's language read thus: "Verily I say unto thee to-day, Thou shalt be with me in Paradise." The meaning then would be, not that the thief would be with him in Paradise on that day, but "I *to-day* say unto thee," etc. Whilst it is, of course, admitted that our punctuation is not of authority, yet we do maintain that the order in which the words stand proves the punctuation correct. No reason, it is believed, can be given to justify the change in the punctuation. Reference is made to Zech. ix. 12 as containing "an expression exactly parallel with that in Luke." It reads thus: "Turn you to the strong hold, ye prisoners of hope: even to-day do I declare that I will render double unto thee." But this is not a parallel case at all, for here the emphatic expression *to-day* precedes the phrase I *declare,* and no one can mistake the meaning. But in the answer of our Lord to the thief, the word *to-day* does not precede but *follows* the words "I say unto thee," thus giving a totally different sense. The objector says: "Transposing this sentence without altering the sense, and we have phraseology similar to that of Luke xxiii. 43." * But you cannot transpose the sentence without altering the sense, for the order of the words determines the sense. So that, whilst all agree as to the meaning of the phraseology in Zech. ix. 12, no respectable commentator or critic, so far as we know, has understood our Lord's language in the same way. The learned Quinöel, referring to the interpretation we are opposing, says it renders the sentence *satis frigida,* sufficiently frigid, and "the very order of the words and the formula, *Verily I say unto thee,* repudiate this conjecture." †

* "Mortal or Immortal," pp. 54–57.

† "Ita vero procederet sententia satis frigida, et ipse

All such attempts to force an unnatural meaning upon the language of Jesus only serve to confirm the obvious interpretation. This one passage, were there no other, is fatal to the doctrine of the mortality and unconscious sleep of the soul, as it is cheering to the heart of the true believer.

3d. The dying prayer of Stephen, the first Christian martyr, is a further refutation of the doctrines under consideration, and a further confirmation of the doctrine of the immortality of the soul. "And they stoned Stephen, calling upon God, and saying, Lord Jesus, receive my spirit." * His body was about to return to the earth as it was; his spirit he committed into the hands of that

verborum ordo, atque formula *αμην λεγω σοι*, hanc conjecturam repudiant." *In loco.*

"But the sublime promise of Christ: *ἀμήν λέγω σοι, σήμερον μετ' ἐμοῦ ἔσῃ ἐν τῷ παραδείσῳ, verily I say unto thee, to-day*, etc., has been superficialized to such a degree by some that they render the words thus: 'I *to-day*' say unto thee," etc.—*Olshausen.*

* Acts vii. 59.

Saviour for whose truth and glory he was laying down his life. There could be no meaning in this dying prayer *if* his spirit was about to die with the body, and both to sleep in "the dust till the resurrection."

But this clear and beautiful petition, like so many other inspired utterances, is to be perverted and obscured by reckless criticism. The word *pneuma* sometimes, though rarely, signifies "the principle of life residing in the breath," and this, we are told, is what Stephen commended to God, to be bestowed upon him again. His life was about to become extinct, and yet we are to believe that he asked Jesus to *receive* that which would no longer exist! And then the prayer, "*Receive my spirit,*" means, "Raise my body, my person, to life at the time of the resurrection!" Is it really necessary to expose such a perversion? "But if the soul lives right along in one uninterrupted course of existence, where," it is asked, "would be the propriety of committing it, at the hour of death, into the hands of our Maker any more than at any other time?"* Suppose there were *no more* propriety in committing the soul to God at the hour of death than at any other time, it will scarcely be pretended that there is *any less* propriety in so doing at so solemn a moment than at any other. Now, since there is eminent propriety in committing one's self to God's keeping at all times, there surely was eminent propriety in Stephen's doing so when dying. But death is the close of man's probation, and "after death the judgment." Is it not pre-eminently proper that the dying servant of God, about to close his probation and to render to God an account of the deeds done in the body, should commit his soul to that Saviour in whom he trusts, and who only can secure to him an entrance into heaven? And is not such a prayer the expression of the earnest longing of the dying believer to go and be with his Lord and Saviour, "whom having

* "Mortal and Immortal," pp. 57, 58.

not seen he loves"? Did not our Saviour himself, in the very same language, commit his spirit, when he was dying, into the hands of his Father? And will it be pretended that his spirit did not continue to live after the death of his body?

It is, then, the inestimable privilege of the believer, when flesh and heart fail, to commit his soul to Him who is the strength of his heart and his portion for ever. It is a precious truth, worth more than all the treasures of earth, that Jesus does receive to himself the souls of his people when they are no longer in the body. How many thousands have sweetly fallen asleep in Christ with this prayer on their lips!

4th. Such was the confidence of the apostles and primitive Christians that immediately after death they would be happy in the presence of their Saviour that they were not only willing but anxious to die. "Therefore," says Paul, "we are always confident, knowing that whilst we are at home in the body we are absent from the Lord. (For we walk by faith, not by sight.) We are confident, I say, and willing rather to be absent from the body, and to be present with the Lord."* The apostle scarcely regarded his body as part of himself, much less as essential to his conscious existence. He speaks of being at home in the body, or absent from it, as one would speak of being in or out of his house. In the same manner Peter speaks of his body as "this tabernacle," which he must soon lay aside.† Such language could never have been used by men who believed either that man is a mere material organism, or that the soul cannot survive separation from the body, or exist consciously in a separate state.

Believers, as Paul here teaches, enjoy "the earnest of the Spirit." In consequence of this, they have an abiding confidence of acceptance with God. And knowing that, so long as they continue in the body, they can-

* 2 Cor. v. 6–8. † 2 Peter i. 14.

not hope to enjoy the immediate and blissful presence of their Redeemer and God, they prefer to leave the body, assured that immediately after death they will be present with him. There is no ambiguity in the apostle's language. It is impossible to doubt, if we are willing to take the plain meaning of the clearest language, that the death of believers—their absence from the body—introduces them immediately into the presence of God, where "there is fullness of joy."

On reading such language one would suppose that no believer in the inspiration of the Scriptures would ever doubt that the soul lives after the death of the body, and that the soul of the believer enjoys a blessed existence. But it is said, by way of objection, that when Paul says he is willing rather to be absent from the body, and to be present with the Lord, "it is certain that his thoughts do not linger in the intermediate state, as if that were to be much prized. He immediately speaks of the scene of judgment."* Is it true, then, that we are to judge of the estimate an inspired writer places upon any of the blessings of redemption by the number of words or sentences he writes about them in any particular chapter? Why did not this writer conclude that the apostle did not regard "the scene of judgment" as a matter of much importance because he immediately passes to other subjects? The question, however, is not *how much*, comparatively, the apostle prized the intermediate state, but what he meant by *being absent from the body, and present with the Lord.* This the writer just quoted interprets thus: "The phrase, 'To be absent from the body,' may therefore denote, not the happiness of a disembodied state, but a release from the suffering and dying body, either to 'sleep in Jesus,' or to be present with Christ in the glorified body of the resurrection." Let us examine this interpretation.

* "Debt and Grace," pp. 255, 256.

1. In the first place, the writer himself is evidently in doubt respecting the meaning of the language he is trying to interpret for the instruction of his readers. He does not pretend to tell us what the apostle *does* mean, but only what he *may* mean. As remarked in a preceding part of this work, this method of argument, if such it may be called, is eminently characteristic of the advocates of the mortality of the soul. There are a number of passages of Scripture which have been almost universally understood by the ablest interpreters, and by the wisest and best men, to teach the immortality of the soul. If the doctrine is not true, these passages have been greatly misunderstood. They certainly have some meaning. We ask earnestly, What *do* they mean? We are answered by these men of extraordinary illumination, who undertake to revolutionize the faith of the Church of Christ, that they *may* mean *this*, or they *may* mean *that*. But we are not satisfied with such answers respecting language which seems

plain and treats of a subject of absorbing interest. We ask not what meaning may be forced upon it, but what *does* it mean? The phrases "absent from the body" and "present with the Lord" cannot be so incomprehensible that sincere inquirers for the truth can only conjecture what they may mean. This method of dealing with such texts is one of the evidences that these men are fighting against truth instead of bringing it to light.

2. The language of Paul, we are told, may mean either of two things as wide apart as the poles. It may, first, mean a release from the suffering and dying body to sleep in Jesus —that is, to lie in a state of death or unconsciousness. If this is the meaning, then the apostle's desire was simply to escape from bodily suffering, and for this end he would gladly pass into an unconscious state, and for the time cease to be. The sentiment is not only unchristian, but unmanly and degrading; and Paul could no more have uttered

it than he could have committed suicide. Moreover, it is a desire which no human being ever felt, unless under extreme distress or in utter despair. But Paul was not only doing a great work for Christ and for the salvation of his fellow-men, but, in spite of all his trials and tribulations, he enjoyed great happiness in his work, in communion with his Saviour and in hope of heaven. He had even learned to "joy in tribulation." Why, then, should he long to lie in the grave in utter unconsciousness? But if being absent from the body was unconscious sleep, what did he mean by being *present with the Lord?* for the two things stand in immediate connection. When absent from the body he would be present with the Lord What does this mean?

Secondly. The apostle's language, we are told, may mean "to be present with Christ in the glorified body of the resurrection." But this sounds strangely. He desired to be absent from the body and to be present in his glorified body. But it must be very perplexing to determine how he could be absent from his body and yet be in his body raised from the grave.

But it really seems like trifling to spend time in exposing such absurdities. It is as clear as light that Paul had in his mind two widely different states in which he might be—viz., in the body and out of the body. Whilst living he was in the body; if he should die he would be out of the body. He preferred to be out of the body. Why? Not because death was in itself a good, or because a disembodied state is in itself preferable to the union of soul and body, but because he had an intense desire to be "present with the Lord"—a privilege he could not enjoy whilst living in the body, but which he would enjoy so soon as he died and was out of the body. Thus is the doctrine proved beyond cavil that the souls of believers are immortal, and do enjoy a conscious and happy existence between death and the resurrection.

5th. In language somewhat different, but equally unambiguous, Paul teaches the same doctrine in the Epistle to the Philippians.* He expresses his earnest desire that Christ might be magnified in his body, whether by life or by death, and then he says, "For me to live is Christ, and to die is gain." To live would be to the honor of Christ, inasmuch as his cause would be promoted by his ministry. To die would be gain to himself, inasmuch as he would rest from his labors and enjoy the blessedness of heaven. Here again we meet with the kind of criticism so characteristic of the advocates of the mortality of the soul. "When he then adds, 'to live is Christ, and to die is gain,' he may signify either the gain to the cause of Christ by the martyrdom which in his person he now awaited, or his own greater reward as a martyr in the resurrection." † That is, we are told that the apostle *may* mean either of two totally different things, but what he *does*

* Phil. i. 20–23. † "Debt and Grace," pp. 256, 257.

mean we are not informed. But Paul explains his meaning, so that we are not left in doubt. He says: "But if I live in the flesh, this is the fruit of my labor, yet what I shall choose, I wot not. For I am in a strait betwixt two, having a desire to depart and to be with Christ, which is far better. Nevertheless, to abide in the flesh is more needful for you." Here observe:

1. The question in his mind was between *abiding in the flesh* and *departing from it.* Not a doubt entered his mind that he might depart from the body as well as continue in it. He evidently did not believe in the doctrine that the soul cannot have a conscious existence out of the body.

2. His desire to depart from the flesh was not that he might be relieved from the sufferings he was called to endure. One of the annihilationist authors tells us that "such were his present afflictions that any form of death would be a welcome release." But, as already remarked, Paul was far from being

unhappy. On the contrary, he not only possessed that elevated joy which true religion never fails to bring to the faithful Christian, especially in times of trial, but he rejoiced to see "that the things which happened to him had fallen out rather unto the furtherance of the gospel."

3. But his desire to depart was *that he might be with Christ*, which he knew to be far better than anything this earth can afford. To die would be to him great gain, because he would be immediately with Christ. But if it be true that the soul lies in an unconscious state from death to the resurrection, what would Paul have gained by dying speedily? How could he have been with Christ any sooner than if he had lived on earth a thousand years? "Measuring the time absolutely," says one of our annihilationist authors, "he could not, to be sure, but measuring it *by his consciousness* (his only means of measurement), and he could just as much sooner as what time elapsed between

the penning of that sentence and the day of his death."* The idea on which these writers insist is, that to one in an unconscious state the interval between death and the resurrection, though of a thousand or ten thousand years' duration, is no more than a moment. "The long and dreary interval, then, between death and the day of judgment (supposing the intermediate state to be a profound sleep) does not exist at all, except in the imagination. To the party concerned there is *no* interval whatever, but to each person (according to this supposition) the moment of his closing his eyes in death will be instantly succeeded by the sound of the last trumpet which shall summon the dead, even though ages shall have intervened."† All this is doubtless true, and it would be just the same on the supposition that a hundred millions of years elapse between death and the resurrection; but it does

* "Mortal or Immortal," p. 65.

† Whateley, "On Future State," pp. 83, 84.

not at all meet the case. We are trying to ascertain why the apostle desired to die rather than to live longer. The reason he assigns is, that he desired to be with Christ. Beyond a question, then, he expected to be with Christ sooner if he died sooner. He expected to be with Christ as soon as he departed from the flesh. But according to the doctrine we are opposing, he would be with Christ just as soon if he lived on earth till the end of time as if he died immediately. Now, let us see what, according to this doctrine, would have been Paul's gain by an early death. Let us suppose that, in accordance with his desire, he had died twenty years sooner than in the course of nature he must have died. What would he have gained? He would not have been one moment sooner with Christ, the object of his heart's desire. What, then, could he have gained? He would have gained *twenty years of unconsciousness!* This would have been precisely his gain, and the whole of it. What would he have lost? He would have lost all his Christian usefulness and all his elevated Christian enjoyment during that period. So that, instead of the earnest desire of a holy man to be with his Saviour, where he could serve him in perfect holiness and enjoy his presence, we have the longing of a man weary of his work and impatient of his trials to pass into a state of insensibility! Can any real Christian, looking at the matter fairly, bring himself to believe that such is the meaning of Paul's language?

Away with all such attempts to wrest the plain language of inspiration from its obvious meaning, and thus to wrest from the believer his glorious hopes! Paul knew that he would be with Christ in glory as soon as he left the body. Therefore it was that he preferred to depart. The doctrine is, therefore, true that the soul, instead of dying with the body, passes into another state of conscious existence, and the souls of believers go to their Redeemer.

CHAPTER VI.

OPPOSING ARGUMENTS CONSIDERED.

ONE of the most plausible arguments in favor of the doctrine of the unconsciousness of the soul between death and the resurrection is the fact that in the Scriptures death is represented as a *sleep*. This argument is urged by Archbishop Whateley, who says: "The style in which the sacred writers usually speak of the deceased is as of persons who are *asleep*." But this argument seems to us to prove just the reverse of that which it is adduced to substantiate; for whilst it is true that in sleep the senses are closed and the body is almost unconscious, this is by no means true of the soul. As we have seen in a preceding part of this work, there is no evidence that at any moment during the deepest sleep it is inactive or unconscious, and we do know that very often it is intensely active and its passions and emotions are profoundly stirred. There are examples of persons having solved mathematical problems whilst asleep which they could not solve when awake. Others have composed music during sleep. Indeed, so far is it from being true that the soul is unconscious in sleep, that God has chosen to make to his servants and to others some of his most important revelations in their dreams. The cases of Pharaoh and Nebuchadnezzar are in point, and it was by a warning conveyed in a dream that the infant Saviour escaped the rage of Herod. "The angel of the Lord appeareth to Joseph in a dream, saying, Arise, and take the young child and his mother and flee into Egypt, and be thou there until I bring thee word; for Herod will seek the young child to destroy him." Again, after the death of Herod, the angel appeared in a dream and bade Joseph return into the land of Israel.

But whilst the soul is evidently always active in sleep, and often most intensely active, it is true that it acts independently of the senses and the bodily organs. It sees without the eyes, hears without the ears, speaks without the tongue. Surely this activity, this intense consciousness of the soul, during the hours of sleep, can afford no proof of that blank unconsciousness, the absolute death of the soul, for which the advocates of its mortality contend. On the contrary, the clearest evidence is thus afforded that it can live and act without the use of the bodily organs. If, then, the inspired writers understood death to be the total unconsciousness of the body, whilst the soul continues conscious and active, they could not employ a more suggestive figure than sleep. Those lines of Young are not only fine poetry, but, like so many of his verses, contain an unanswerable argument:

"'Tis past conjecture, all things rise in proof;
While o'er my limbs sleep's soft dominion spread,

What though my soul fantastic measures trod
O'er fairy fields, or mourn'd along the gloom
Of pathless woods, or, down the craggy steep
Hurl'd headlong, swam with pain the mantled pool,
Or scal'd the cliff, or danc'd on hollow winds,
With antic shapes, wild natives of the brain?
Her ceaseless flight, though devious, speaks her nature
Of subtler essence than the trodden clod,
Active, aerial, tow'ring, unconfin'd,
Unfetter'd with her gross companion's fall.
E'en silent night proclaims my soul immortal,
E'en silent night proclaims eternal day.
For human weal heaven husbands all events:
Dull sleep instructs, nor sport vain dreams in vain."

Death is represented as a sleep, doubtless, because it is not the destruction of the person for even a temporary period, the soul still living and acting, and because even the death of the body is to be temporary. The period of death is but a night; God will, in due time, awaken the slumbering dust. "Our friend Lazarus sleepeth," said Jesus, "but I go, that I may awake him out of sleep." And so Daniel says of all the dead: "And many of them (or the multitude of them) that sleep in the dust of the earth shall awake."

The two great events, the resurrection and a general judgment, it is well remarked, are "fixed facts." From these two great facts two arguments are offered to prove that the soul dies with the body.

1. The first argument is stated thus: "What need is there of a resurrection if the man proper ceases not to exist at death, but lives on in a more enlarged and perfect sphere of consciousness and activity? If the body is but a trammel, a clog, to the operations of the soul, what need that it should come back and gather up its scattered particles from the silent tomb?" * This argument, if it deserves the name, is easily answered.

In the first place, the body is not a mere trammel to the soul, a clog to its operations, but an organism without which its peculiar mission in this world could not be accomplished. It becomes a clog only as it is

* "Mortal or Immortal," p. 84.

abused by unlawful indulgence, or as its powers decay under the sentence of death.

In the second place, though the souls of the righteous do rise at death to a higher sphere of conscious activity, yet their bodies, as raised from the dead, may, and doubtless will, add greatly to their happiness and fit them for their peculiar mission in a brighter world. If it were admitted that since the introduction of sin and death into the world the body has become a clog to the soul, it would not follow that when purified and refined by the power of God at the resurrection, it will continue to be so. "It is sown in dishonor, it is raised in glory; it is sown in weakness, it is raised in power; it is sown a natural body, it is raised a spiritual body." "For this corruptible must put on incorruption, and this mortal must put on immortality." * For Jesus Christ "shall change our vile body, that it may be fashioned like unto his glorious body, according to the work-

* 1 Cor. xv. 42–44, 53.

ing whereby he is able even to subdue all things unto himself." * Let it be admitted that "our vile body" is a clog to the soul: does it follow that our *glorious* body will be so? As much more refined than the present body as light is more refined than the earth on which we tread, no longer possessing ensnaring appetites, no longer subject to disease or decay, it will be a tabernacle suited to the work and the enjoyments of the sanctified spirit. Therefore the saints wait for "the redemption of their body." †

Thus, moreover, it will appear that sin has triumphed over no part of man—that the whole man, body and soul, has been rescued by the Redeemer from its iron grasp. "So when this corruptible shall have put on incorruption, and this mortal shall have put on immortality, then shall be brought to pass the saying that is written, Death is swallowed up in victory. O Death, where is thy sting? O Grave, where is thy victory?"‡

* Phil. iii. 21. † Rom. viii. 23. ‡ 1 Cor. xv. 54, 55.

Having answered the argument sought to be derived from the resurrection against the immortality of the soul, we now derive from this same doctrine an argument of great weight in favor of its immortality, viz.: that although *the person* is frequently said to die and to rise from the dead, yet the inspired writers repeatedly explain that it is only the *body*, not the *soul*, that is to be raised from the dead. Thus it is said that at the resurrection of our Lord "the graves were opened, many dead BODIES of the saints which slept arose, and came out of the graves."* Paul says: "If the Spirit of Him that raised up Jesus from the dead dwell in you, He that raised up Christ from the dead shall also quicken your MORTAL BODIES by his Spirit that dwelleth in you."† And again: "Who shall change our VILE BODY, that it may be fashioned like unto his glorious body."‡ Now, this language is perfectly intelligible and consistent on the supposition that the soul sur-

* Matt. xxvii. 52. † Rom. viii. 11. ‡ Phil. iii. 21.

vives the body, or passes into another state of conscious existence, but it is utterly unaccountable on the supposition that the whole man, soul and body, lies in the grave, and is raised from the dead. The Scriptures do constantly speak of both the soul and the body with reference to death and the future state, and they speak distinctly of the resurrection of *the body*, but in not an instance do they mention the resurrection of *the soul.* Why is this? It is the body, not the soul, that is to be quickened; it is the body, not the soul, that is to be fashioned like unto the glorified body of Christ. The reason is obvious: it is the body, not the soul, that dies.

2. The argument for the mortality of the soul derived from the general judgment is stated thus: "What propriety can there be in a general judgment at the last day, if those who pass from this state of existence enter immediately at death into happiness or misery, accordingly as their characters have been good or bad? Is there possibility of mis-

take in the decision passed upon some at death, and is it perhaps the case that some have been unjustly tormented in hell and others unworthily reveling in the bliss of heaven for ages past, so that there must needs be a general assize on the whole human race to correct these momentous errors of former decisions? Such a view reflects on the character of the divine government."* This argument is founded on the supposition that a general judgment is necessary in order that God the Judge may ascertain accurately the true characters of individuals and assign them their proper place of happiness or punishment. But this is absurd. And may we not ask, if this is the true view, why there should be a general judgment at all, since it is certain that the all-wise Judge knows as well before as afterward the true character of every human being?

But suppose the general judgment designed to vindicate the divine administration of the

* "Mortal or Immortal," pp. 84, 85.

affairs of this world before the intelligent universe, to glorify, in the highest degree, the Triune God, and to make a profound and happy moral impression upon men and angels. Such an object would constitute the reason why it is to occur at the end of the world, when the great plan shall have been completed and the grand results could be made manifest. Then, those parts of the divine procedure which have been too deep and too high for the comprehension of the wisest and best men, and which have led wicked men to blaspheme the name of God, will shine forth to the admiring joy of saints and angels, and to the confusion of the ungodly.

This is the view constantly set forth in the Scriptures. The Apostle Paul teaches that the plan of salvation is developed "to the intent that now unto the principalities and powers in heavenly places might be known, by the church, the manifold wisdom of God, according to the eternal purpose which he purposed in Christ Jesus our Lord." * But there are many things in this wonderful plan which, to the angels to whom the apostle refers, are yet profoundly mysterious, and which they cannot comprehend, and "the manifold wisdom" of which they cannot see till it shall be completed. "Which things," says Peter, "the angels desire to look into." † Therefore the Psalmist, speaking of the general judgment, says: "He shall call to the heavens from above, and to the earth, that he may judge his people. Gather my saints together unto me, those that have made a covenant with me by sacrifice. And the heavens shall declare his righteousness, for God is judge himself." ‡ He issues his summons to the inhabitants of heaven and earth to witness the solemn scene, that the heavens may declare his righteousness. Accordingly, we read that "when the Son of man shall come in his glory," the holy angels shall come with him, to witness

* Eph. iii. 9–11. † 1 Pet. i. 12. ‡ Ps. l. 4–6.

the final adjudication.* And Paul tells us that he "shall be revealed from heaven with his mighty angels, in flaming fire, taking vengeance on them that know not God, and that obey not the gospel of our Lord Jesus Christ," and that "he shall come to be glorified in his saints, and to be admired in all them that believe." †

In no part of the Scriptures do we find the absurd idea that the general judgment is designed to enable God to determine the characters of men, or even to enable men to know their own characters. It is designed to vindicate the divine administration, and to make known to the intelligent universe the manifold wisdom of God in the plan of salvation. The doctrine of a general judgment, therefore, affords not the slightest evidence of the mortality of the soul.

A third argument, drawn from these two doctrines, and much insisted on, is that it is at the resurrection, not before, that the saints

* Matt. xxv. 31, 32 † 2 Thess. i. 7–10.

are to receive their reward. For example, those who are kind to the poor are to be recompensed "at the resurrection of the just." Again, "And when the chief Shepherd shall appear, ye shall receive a crown of glory that fadeth not away." Now, it is true that the saints of God are taught to look to the morning of the resurrection as the period when, by the deliverance of their bodies from death, their redemption will be completed; and it is true that it is when the whole man, soul and body, shall stand before God, that Jesus Christ will acknowledge his redeemed ones before his Father and the holy angels, and bestow upon them their full reward. That will be their coronation day. But to infer from all this that between death and the resurrection the soul is in an unconscious state is most illogical. The purposes to be answered by the general judgment, as already explained, require that the day of judgment should be the period when the reward of the righteous will be announced and the sentence of the wicked proclaimed.

That the soul dies with the body is demonstrated, it is said, because Paul "declares that unless he (man) comes forth again from the grave he is perished, that is the end of him, he is irrecoverably and for ever gone." But the apostle says no such thing. He is proving the fact that Christ is risen from the dead, and he argues thus: "For if the dead rise not, then is not Christ raised, and if Christ be not raised, your faith is vain, ye are yet in your sins. Then they also which are fallen asleep in Christ are perished." * The argument is this: All men are sinners, and therefore they are under the curse of the broken law. Now, if Christ is not risen, this fact proves that he is not the Saviour of men. Consequently, his disciples are yet in their sins, their faith being vain, and those of them who have died, died in their sins, and have perished under the curse. But the ob-

* 1 Cor. xv. 16–18.

jector *assumes* that the word "*perished*" means annihilation; for if it means, as generally understood, endless punishment, it affords no evidence whatever in favor of the mortality of the soul. One of the ablest living critics explains the apostle's language thus: "Perdition, according to Scripture, is not annihilation, but everlasting misery and sin. It is the loss of holiness and happiness for ever. If Christ did not rise for the justification of those who died in him, they found no advocate at the bar of God, and have incurred the fate of those who perish in their sins." * The meaning of this important word (*perished*) will be carefully considered in the course of this discussion.

One of the most plausible arguments for the mortality of the soul is an inference from the language of Paul to the Thessalonians: "But I would not have you to be ignorant, brethren, concerning them which are asleep, that ye sorrow not, even as others which

* Dr. Hodge *in loco.*

have no hope. For if we believe that Jesus died and rose again, even so them also which sleep in Jesus will God bring with him." * Paul, it is urged, comforted the Thessalonian Christians, not with the assurance that their deceased friends were already in heaven, but that they would rise from the dead, and then be for ever with the Lord. But "popular ministers," it is said, do not comfort mourners in this way, but by telling them their friends are *now* in glory. The inference is that Paul did not believe that deceased Christians do enjoy a happy existence before the resurrection. To all of which we answer:

1. That we never find the inspired writers comforting believers, as do the annihilationists, by assuring them that to their deceased friends and to themselves the interval between death and the resurrection, however long it may really be, will appear but a moment. Now, if the inference is legitimate that they did not believe what is called "the popular

* 1 Thess. iv. 13, 14.

doctrine" because they did not comfort mourners in the way adopted by "the popular preachers," may we not as justly conclude that they did not believe the annihilationist doctrine because they did not comfort mourners as do annihilationists? Wise men never employ arguments against the faith of others which are fatal to their own.

2. In the apostolic age the two doctrines, the immortality of the soul and the resurrection, were close companions. There were, indeed, those amongst the Gentiles who knew nothing of the resurrection who believed the soul immortal, for the doctrine of the resurrection is purely a doctrine of Revelation, but we know of none who believed the doctrine of the resurrection of the body who denied the immortality of the soul. "For," says Luke, "the Sadducees say that there is no resurrection, neither angel nor spirit, but the Pharisees confess both." * Each of these Jewish sects was consistent with itself. The

* Acts xxiii. 8.

Sadducees were materialists. Denying the immortality of the soul, they also denied the resurrection of the body, and they likewise denied the existence of disembodied spirits. The Pharisees, holding to the immortality of the soul, believed also the resurrection of the body, and they admitted the existence of spirits. Annihilationists are chargeable with the inconsistency of attempting to separate these kindred doctrines.

Such being the forms of religious belief in the days of Christ and his apostles, it is evident that when the doctrine of the resurrection was proved the doctrine of the immortality of the soul followed of course.

And now we can see the force of our Lord's refutation of the Sadducees: "But as touching the resurrection of the dead, have ye not read that which was spoken unto you by God, saying, I am the God of Abraham, and the God of Isaac, and the God of Jacob? God is not the God of the dead, but of the living." * This argument demonstrated that, though the bodies of Abraham, Isaac and Jacob had long been dead, they themselves were living. It put the Sadducees to silence. Why? They denied two great doctrines of Revelation, viz.: the immortality of the soul and the resurrection of the body, and their rejection of the latter doctrine was a consequence of their disbelief of the former. Jesus Christ knew this, and therefore he struck at the *proton pseudos*—the radical error. He knew that if they were convinced of the immortality of the soul, they would find no difficulty in admitting the resurrection of the dead. He therefore demonstrated the immortality of the soul by proving that Abraham, Isaac and Jacob were yet alive. Thus the conclusiveness of his argument is clear, and we are not under the necessity, as the annihilationists are, of forcing upon his language a most unnatural meaning, viz.: that God is the God of those who are dead, but

* Matt. xxii. 31, 32.

not the God of "those who are *irrecoverably and eternally dead.*"

Now, then, we can see why Paul comforted believers concerning their departed friends by pointing them to the resurrection, for this doctrine implied the immortality of the soul. No one who believed the former doctrine denied the latter. If those who had fallen asleep in Christ were to rise again, it followed that their souls were now happy with him. The apostle, therefore, fixed their minds upon the completion of their redemption, the final triumph, when the whole redeemed family, those who had died and those who would be alive at the resurrection, would ascend together and be for ever with the Lord. The inference, therefore, that the apostle held that the soul dies with the body is wholly unwarranted.

CHAPTER VII.

THE FINAL DESTINY OF THE WICKED.

WHAT do the Scriptures teach respecting the final destiny of the wicked?

We now come to the last question proposed for discussion. On two points the annihilationists agree with us, viz.: 1. That the wicked as well as the righteous will be raised from the dead. 2. That after being raised the righteous will receive their reward and the wicked will endure the penalty due to their sins. But they maintain what we deny—that the punishment of the wicked will be annihilation, or will end in annihilation.

That "the wages of sin is death" Paul distinctly teaches.* Whether *death* means

* Rom. vi. 23.

the extinction of *being*, or the extinction of *hope* and consequent *endless suffering*, is the question to be determined. This has been a fruitful theme for abstract reasoning and speculation, respecting which we may say, as Gibbon says of the speculations of pagan philosophers concerning the divine nature, that "in the profound inquiry they displayed the strength and the weakness of the human understanding." The divine purposes concerning the righteous and the wicked involve questions too high and too deep for human reason, and, with infinite interests at stake, we desire to plant our feet on a more solid foundation. Let us, therefore, come directly to the light of God's word, without wearying our minds with the speculations, more or less plausible, by which men have undertaken to prove that moral evil must or must not continue for ever.

In the twenty-fifth chapter of Matthew we have presented before us by Christ himself a panoramic view of the general judgment, and there we learn, in language remarkably clear, what is to be the destiny both of the righteous and of the wicked. The Son of man is to come in his glory, and all the holy angels with him. All nations are to be gathered before him, and he will separate them from each other as a shepherd divideth the sheep from the goats. To the righteous he will say, "Come, ye blessed of my Father, inherit the kingdom prepared for you from the foundation of the world." To the wicked he will say, "Depart from me, ye cursed, into everlasting fire, prepared for the devil and his angels." The final result is announced thus: "And these shall go away into everlasting punishment, but the righteous into life eternal."

The question respecting the destiny of the wicked, so far as this passage is concerned, turns upon the two words, "everlasting punishment." With Universalists the controversy relates to the meaning of the word *everlasting*. They contend for a limited meaning. Hudson and other annihilationist writers "waive all argument in behalf of a limited sense of the word 'everlasting,'" though they do not fail to tell us that "a very strong case could be made out for such a sense." * No one denies that the word here translated *everlasting* is sometimes used to signify a limited period, but such a meaning can be forced on the word here only by the utter disregard of the rules of language. The same Greek word which expresses the duration of the life of the righteous expresses the duration of the punishment of the wicked. If, then, the former is unlimited, so is the latter.

But annihilationists join issue on the word *punishment*, and the question they raise is this: "Does it necessarily denote *conscious pain?*" They insist that it means nothing more than "eternal privation of being," or annihilation. "The difficulty, we apprehend," says one of them, "arises from confounding

* "Debt and Grace," p. 187.

punishment with conscious suffering, whereas it is not necessarily such. Mark where the antithesis occurs: it is between life and punishment. . . . We therefore plead for the plain and literal import of the terms. Life, then, means life, and life here is just the opposite of the punishment brought to view." * Another writer adopts a different exposition. All those in the scene, he thinks, "are professed Christians—the true and the false, the genuine and the hypocrites. They are together called 'all the nations.' These words are not intended to mean all mankind, but are designed to be commensurate with the words in the apostolic commission, 'Go ye, therefore, and disciple all nations.'" Thus he disposes of the phrase, "all nations." The ideal meaning of the word *kolasin*, translated *punishment*, he further informs us, "is *to take from, to cut off*, and hence to prune or to cut off unfruitful or worthless branches from a tree which is itself a good tree. And

* "Mortal or Immortal," p. 94.

kolazo is the Greek equivalent of the Hebrew KAH-RATH, which means to cut off as a branch is cut off, and to cut off by death, and is used when it is said, 'That soul shall be cut off,' 'that soul shall be cut off from Israel.' Even so the false Christians shall be cut off from the flock of Christ, and from every pretence to the kingdom, of which they were *ostensible* heirs, in common with the true, and their excision shall not be temporal, but shall be *eternal.*" *

These writers give us two interpretations of this important passage. The one makes the word translated *punishment* mean *excision*, the others make it mean *privation*. Let us examine both of these interpretations.

That the word does not mean *excision*, or the separation of hypocrites from true believers, is clear from several considerations.

1. It requires a most extraordinary and arbitrary interpretation of the phrase, "all nations." This phrase is indeed "commen-

* "Quest. of Ages," p. 98.

surate with the words in the apostolic commission.". But those words mean the same as those recorded by Mark: "Go ye into all the world, and preach the gospel to every creature." The commission embraces all the world, and so will the general judgment. To make the phrase, "all nations," mean only the professing Christians of all nations is a most unwarrantable perversion of language.

2. If we were to admit that the word translated *punishment* sometimes means *excision,* it is clear that such is not its meaning in the passage under consideration. For although we constantly meet, in the Old Testament, with such expressions as, *To be cut off from my people,* yet in no instance is it said that offenders *shall go away into excision.* Nor would the expression, *eternal excision,* be less extraordinary. No writer would employ such expressions to signify the separation of unworthy persons from the church. It is not only an incorrect, but a ridiculous, use of language.

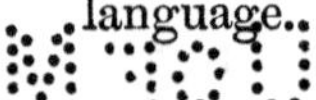

3. The word *kolasin* never has the meaning which this writer attaches to it. The verb *kolazo* sometimes signifies *to prune;* and if the church were spoken of, in this view of the general judgment, as a *tree*, there might be some appearance of propriety in resorting to this meaning. But the scene presented is that of a king on his throne, summoning before him his subjects that he may suitably reward the faithful and inflict merited punishment upon the rebellious. In such a connection no one would think of using a word signifying *pruning.* There would be as much propriety in talking of the *pruning* or *excision* of a criminal in court. Dr. Morris tells us that *kolazo* is the Greek equivalent of the Hebrew KAH-RATH, which is used when it is said, "That soul shall be cut off." But the conclusive proof that this statement is incorrect is the fact, which he should have known, that, often as this expression occurs in the law of Moses, the Hebrew word KAH-RATH is never translated in the Septuagint

by the Greek *kolazo*. If the latter were the equivalent of the former, why was it never used as the translation of it?

4. The constant and the uniform usage of the word *kolasin* proves that it signifies *punishment* in the proper sense of the word. Hudson, after quoting a number of passages in the Old Testament and in the Apocryphal books in which this word occurs, remarks: "The ethical sense of 'punishment,' as distinct from calamity or mere excision, is apparent in all the passages. The same is true of its usage in the New Testament." The verb *kolazo* occurs in Acts iv. 21, where it is said, the Jewish council, after threatening the apostles, let them go, "finding nothing how they might punish (*kolasontai*) them." It occurs again in 2 Pet. ii. 9, where it is said, the Lord knoweth how to reserve "the unjust unto the day of judgment to be punished (*kolazomenous*)." The noun *kolasis* occurs in 1 John iv. 18, where it is translated *torment*, and signifies that suffering which is caused

by guilty fear. The usage of the word, then, shows the correctness of our translation. The word means *punishment.* The context proves the same theory. The glorious King comes to judge and reward his subjects. In order to this, he divides them into two classes, according to their characters. The righteous he rewards, the wicked he punishes. And what else can be intended by the sentence, "Depart from me, ye cursed, into everlasting fire, prepared for the devil and his angels"? What is the meaning of "*everlasting fire*"?

There remains but one more question to be determined in relation to this important passage, viz.: Whether the punishment consists in endless suffering, or in annihilation. It is said, the punishment is the antithesis of *life,* and therefore must be understood to be *annihilation.* This might be true if the word *life* here signified merely conscious existence. In that case the antithesis would be non-existence or annihilation. But the word *life* is evidently here used, as constantly in the

New Testament, in the sense of *holy* and *happy existence.* The language of our Lord in John v. 24 makes the meaning clear: "Verily I say unto you, He that heareth my word, and believeth on Him that sent me, hath everlasting life, and shall not come into condemnation, but is passed from death unto life." When it is said of the believer that he is passed from death unto life, the meaning is not that he has passed from non-existence to conscious existence, but from a state of sin and condemnation to a holy, justified state. He has entered upon a holy and happy life which shall be endless. If, then, the eternal life of the righteous is to be a holy and happy existence, the antithesis of this would be, not annihilation, but a *sinful, unhappy existence.*

This meaning of the word *kolasin* is required by the word *everlasting*, which qualifies it. Doubtless, God, if he chose, could with infinite ease annihilate the wicked on account of their sins, and annihilation, inflicted on an immortal being, would certainly be a punishment, but in no possible sense could it be *everlasting*. Punishment, whether it be of the nature of privation or of positive suffering, can be inflicted only on a being who is conscious of it, and it requires no argument to prove that it cannot continue after the subject of it has ceased to exist. To say that it can is to maintain the possibility of punishing *nothing*, which is absurd. Still clearer, if possible, is it that annihilation, inflicted upon a *mortal* being, could not be everlasting punishment, for it could only hasten an event which must occur in the course of nature. Consequently, it could only deprive him of a limited, not an everlasting, existence. The fact that immortality was offered to him, but not accepted, does not alter the case, for since he never possessed immortality, he could not be *deprived* of it.

The conclusive evidence that we have given to the phrase "everlasting punishment" its true meaning is the fact that it must have been so understood by those to whom our

Lord was speaking. Amongst the Jews there were but two views respecting the future state, the one held by the Sadducees, the other by the Pharisees. The Sadducees, as we learn from both Josephus and the New Testament, believed that the souls of men die with their bodies, and they rejected the doctrine of the resurrection. They were, therefore, annihilationists, though differing materially from those of our day. The Pharisees believed in the immortality of the soul, in the resurrection of the just and the unjust, and in the endless punishment of the wicked. "They also believe," says Josephus, "that souls have an immortal vigor in them, and that under the earth there will be rewards or punishments, according as they have lived virtuously or viciously in this life, and the latter are to be detained in an everlasting prison," etc. When, therefore, our Lord spoke of everlasting punishment to be inflicted on the wicked after the resurrection, his disciples, unless informed to the contrary, must have understood him to teach the doctrine held by all the Jews except the Sadducees. If the modern doctrine of the annihilation of the wicked at a period succeeding the resurrection had ever been known amongst the Jews, it had certainly disappeared before the advent of Christ. If, therefore, he had designed to teach it, and to correct the prevailing belief, he most certainly would not have employed language so likely to confirm the existing faith, and which, on this supposition, has misled ninety-nine hundredths of the readers of the New Testament from that day to this.

That the punishment of the wicked will not be merely that of *privation*, "cutting off from life," but positive suffering, we are distinctly taught by the Apostle Paul. After saying that God "will render to every man according to his deeds" at the day of judgment, he thus describes the destiny of the righteous and of the wicked respectively: "To them who by patient continuance in well-doing seek for glory and honor and immortality, eternal life; but unto them that are contentious, and do not obey the truth, but obey unrighteousness, indignation and wrath, tribulation and anguish, upon every soul that doeth evil." * The doom of the wicked is to be the suffering of the indignation and wrath of God, inflicting tribulation and anguish. It is certain that these words, "tribulation and anguish," do express positive suffering. This the apostle declares to be the penalty the wicked shall suffer, but not the slightest intimation does he give either that the penalty is the privation of conscious existence or that it will terminate in this. But as he is here expressly teaching what is the penalty of sin, he could not have failed to speak of annihilation if this had been the penalty.

This doctrine is further proved by our Saviour's language in John iii. 36: "He that believeth on the Son hath everlasting life, and he that believeth not on the Son

* Rom. ii. 7-10.

shall not see life, but the wrath of God abideth on him." Believers now possess and shall enjoy eternal life—a life of holiness and bliss—but unbelievers not only shall not enjoy eternal life, but instead of this, the wrath of God shall abide on them. Now, it is certain that the wrath of God cannot abide on *nothing;* it cannot, therefore, abide on beings who no longer exist. Most certainly, then, the wicked will continue to exist and to suffer under the divine displeasure. But says Hudson, "The state of death was deemed by the Jews an evil. And by a natural dramatism, the subtlety of thoughts ever transcending the subtlety of words, such a destiny might be expressed in language which, grammatically taken, implies existence." He acknowledges that our Lord's language, grammatically taken, implies the continued existence of the wicked; how, then, is the language to be made to convey a meaning directly the reverse of its plain, grammatical meaning? Interpreted according to the established principles of language, it confessedly teaches the continued existence of the wicked; but we are to imagine a fiction called "a natural dramatism," and to suppose that the subtlety of the thoughts which our Lord was endeavoring to communicate transcends the subtlety of his language, and then we may suppose that he meant just the reverse of that which he said! He said the wicked continue to exist: he meant that they cease to exist! In the hands of such critics language ceases to be the medium of ideas, and becomes a mere plaything. These gentlemen find no difficulty in giving expression to their faith in plain, unambiguous language. Could not our Saviour do the same?

The doctrine of the endless punishment of the wicked is further confirmed by the punishment denounced against blasphemy against the Holy Spirit: "But he that shall blaspheme against the Holy Ghost hath never forgiveness, but is in danger of eternal damnation." This, we are told, means "a judgment or condemnation, the effects of which will be eternal." Agreed. But what are the effects of condemnation? They are the sufferings to which the criminals are condemned, and, therefore, *eternal* condemnation must mean endless sufferings. Thus "eternal salvation" (Heb. v. 9) is a salvation the happy effects of which are to be eternally experienced by its subjects. "Eternal redemption" (Heb. ix. 12) is a redemption the blissful fruits of which are to be for ever enjoyed. "The everlasting gospel" (Rev. xiv. 6) is a gospel whose blessings are to be for ever possessed. A "perpetual covenant" (Ex. xxxi. 16) is a covenant designed to be perpetually in force. Such is the uniform usage of the Scriptures. The penalty of sin might have been annihilation, but in no possible sense could such a sentence be called *an eternal condemnation.* One might as well speak of a stroke of lightning as continuing half a century, because it killed a child that might have lived fifty years, as of an eternal condemnation to annihilation. Such language is not merely extraordinary, it is unheard of.

There are many other passages of Scripture that might be cited in refutation of the doctrine of the annihilation of the wicked. Perhaps some passages to which we have not referred may be thought to present evidence quite as strong as those we have quoted. But we are willing to close the argument at this point, for we are persuaded that the evidence we have adduced is abundantly sufficient to satisfy the unprejudiced, and we know full well that no language, however clear or strong, can convince those whose minds are blinded by prejudice.

The great question, then, which God has submitted to men, is not whether they will continue to live or cease to exist, but whether their future life shall be holy and happy or sinful and wretched. Depraved and degraded men may say, "Let us eat and drink, for to-morrow we die." Or in the vain effort to escape from the wretchedness which their sins have brought upon them they may commit suicide, as so many are doing. But the Creator has imparted to the soul a life which is indestructible. If, as our Saviour declared, the murderer who kills his victim cannot kill his soul, neither can the suicide destroy its life. It is a glorious and a fearful truth that every human being has entered upon an existence which is destined to run parallel with that of God, and through the endless ages every one must glorify the *grace* or the *justice* of God. We must act, then, under the pressure of eternal motives; and the question we are settling is, whether we will lay up treasure in heaven, or treasure up wrath against the day of wrath. We are obliged to live, form character and receive reward. What character we will form, and what shall be our reward, are the questions we are now settling. May God give us wisdom to choose!

The doctrine we have now proved is full of consolation and joy to the children of

God. They are no mere material organisms governed by material laws, incapable alike of virtue or vice, but *spirits* possessed of free moral agency, capable of bearing the image of their glorious Creator. This short life is not to be followed by a long, dreary night of unconsciousness, but the putting off their frail tabernacle will introduce them immediately into the presence of their Saviour, and into the bliss of heaven. "And I heard a voice from heaven saying unto me, Write, Blessed are the dead that die in the Lord from henceforth: yea, saith the Spirit, that they may rest from their labors; and their works do follow them." Rev. xiv. 13.

www.ingramcontent.com/pod-product-compliance
Lightning Source LLC
LaVergne TN
LVHW011222110826
845150LV00006B/1505